The Return of the Public

The Return of the Public

DAN HIND

VERSO

London • New York

First published by Verso 2010
© Dan Hind 2010

The moral rights of the author have been asserted

1 3 5 7 9 10 8 6 4 2

Verso
UK: 6 Meard Street, London W1F 0EG
US: 20 Jay Street, Suite 1010, Brooklyn, NY 11201
www.versobooks.com

Verso is the imprint of New Left Books

ISBN-13: 978-1-84467-594-4

British Library Cataloguing in Publication Data
A catalogue record for this book is available from the British Library

Library of Congress Cataloging-in-Publication Data
A catalog record for this book is available from the Library of Congress

Typeset in Perpetua by Hewer Text UK Ltd, Edinburgh
Printed and bound in Great Britain by CPI Mackays

The aristocrats of intelligence find that there are truths which should not be told to the people. As a revolutionary socialist, and a sworn enemy of all aristocracies and all tutelage, I believe to the contrary that the people must be told everything. There is no other way to restore them to their full liberty.

Mikhail Bakunin

Contents

Part 3: The Return of the Public

Introduction

In a democracy public opinion is sovereign
Alexis de Tocqueville

FOR THE LAST 30 years American and British politicians have allowed powerful economic interests to manage their own affairs. Whether liberal, nominally social democratic or conservative, successive governments assured voters that their surrender to market forces served the public interest. Once freed from an intrusive state, self-interested investors would identify economic opportunities and deliver faster economic growth. Privatized companies would become dynamic and efficient. Finance could be left to regulate itself, while government became more business-like.[1] The majority would benefit from government's refusal to restrain market forces or to take action in the economy: whatever investors wanted was good for growth and so, by definition, was in the common interest.

In the summer of 2007 the financial markets, which had epitomized the way that private self-interest was supposed to deliver public goods, began to seize up. In the months and years that followed, governments around the world, led by the United States and Britain, committed billions to rescue failing financial institutions and lent billions more at very low levels of interest. The working majority, having been told for a generation that deregulated finance would bring them their hearts' desires, discovered that they were suddenly liable for huge new debts. Though the profits of the preceding decades went disproportionately to the wealthy, the losses belonged

1

to everyone. The financial sector had justified its vast profits as the fruits of prudent risk-taking in competitive markets. It was now clear that their private gains had accrued from the reckless exploitation of a public guarantee.

For a while, the bankruptcy of the conventional wisdom could be discussed openly. Speaking in October 2008 Alan Greenspan, the former head of the Federal Reserve, acknowledged that 'the whole intellectual edifice' for managing risk in the vast global market for derivatives had collapsed in the summer of the previous year.[2] Greenspan admitted that he had found a 'flaw' in the ideology that had guided him during his tenure at the Federal Reserve:

> I don't know how significant or permanent it is. But I have been very distressed by that fact . . . I made a mistake in presuming that the self-interests of organisations, specifically banks and others, were such that they were best capable of protecting their own shareholders and their equity in the firms.[3]

By the time the financial crisis broke, the ideology that guided Greenspan at the Federal Reserve had spread throughout the state administration. In Michael Sandel's words, 'for three decades, the governing philosophy of the United States and Britain was defined by the faith that markets are the primary instrument for achieving the public good'.[4] When Samuel Brittan wrote that 'all provision for the consumer on a competitive basis in a non-distorted market is a public service', he was doing no more than stating the prevailing delirium.[5] Those who doubted the power of self-interest to prevent systemic collapse struggled to be heard in an intellectual edifice that, though gimcrack, had been lavishly soundproofed by Greenspan and his friends in finance, academia and the media.

We have been through a severe recession and are now being told by Larry Summers, one of Barack Obama's senior economic advisors and a partner of Greenspan in the deregulation of finance, that we can look forward to 'a statistical recovery and a human recession'. Summers explains that higher levels of unemployment are a structural feature of the US economy and will not fall when the business cycle turns.[6] Many of those who have lost their jobs will not find new ones. Meanwhile the financial markets are demanding cuts in state expenditure to reduce ballooning fiscal deficits. Even a statistical recovery is in jeopardy. The financial markets' demands that governments cut deficits while leaving the rich only lightly taxed will weaken demand and may even choke off the recent return to growth.

The events of 2007 and the ensuing shambles should have put to rest the interconnected assumptions that defined and limited our sense of what was politically and economically possible. They should have emboldened us to consider what it would mean to live in a functioning democracy and to discuss the reforms that are needed if we are to avoid the grotesque future mapped out for us and for our children, in which we struggle under the burden of debts to which we did not consent, the consequence of a crisis we did not cause. The arguments used to deny the general population a meaningful role in shaping policy fell apart when private self-interest drove the financial system to the point of collapse and state intervention saved it. Those who, for a generation, dominated the management of the economy, and hence the substance of politics, should no longer be allowed to set the terms of the debate.

Yet as I write most of us can only watch as the architects of the old order insist on their right to remain in control while denying that they might be responsible for the crisis they caused. In former Treasury Secretary Hank Paulson's words, we are all on the hook 'for the system we all let happen'.[7] So now we must reduce the deficit to restore the animal spirits of the financial markets. There has been little open debate about how the deficit is to be reduced. The glut of capital in the offshore system remains weirdly invisible to most mainstream commentators and the interlocking claims and descriptions that constitute the global media have survived more or less intact.

The dizzying inequality, the gigantic infrastructure of military power, the deepening social and environmental problems, all remain beyond the reach of democratic debate. We are expected to pay up and keep quiet.

The peoples of Britain and the United States are now on the hook for more than 13 trillion dollars ($13,000,000,000,000). Money borrowed to rescue the banks has joined vast sums spent on weapons procurement and the steady enrichment of contractors against a background of escalating tax avoidance and evasion by the very rich.[8] This book sets out the terms on which we should accept responsibility for these debts after a generation of fairy tales, close confinement and abuse. The current economic crisis should be seen as an opportunity to revise the ways in which we engage with powerful economic institutions, with the state and with one another.

The book contributes to this process of revision in three ways. Firstly, it sets out how we have tended to construe the idea of the public. A clear understanding of what it means to act in a public capacity and to engage in public life is central to a properly political identity. The current definitions of the public and the assumptions that shaped them have helped bring us to our current condition. Yet our sense of what the word means is often confused and contradictory. In ordinary speech we contrast the private world of family and friends with the world outside, the public world of strangers. Yet the 'public sector' – that is, the state – and the 'private sector' – that is, business – are both 'public' in this first sense. In the last three centuries production has expanded beyond the household and made it seem natural to think of the economy as an aspect of public life in a way that would have been wholly alien to earlier generations.

The idea of the public does not always become clearer in academic writing. Some theorists, such as David Marquand and Ralf Dahrendorff, attach considerable importance to a 'public realm' that combines the state and charitable and philanthropic institutions and is distinct from, indeed stands in opposition to, both commercial and familial relationships. On the other hand an influential tradition associated with Jürgen Habermas emphasizes the role that private citizens connected by markets played in creating the eighteenth-century 'public sphere'.[9]

Early modern writers talked of a select group of 'public men', who owed their status to royal patronage. In the seventeenth century in Britain resistance to the monarchy drew on classical republicanism and argued for government by an active public of citizens. Individuals could only count themselves free, fully human even, if they exerted direct control of the state. Later, as candid republicanism gave way to oligarchic discretion and the appearance of monarchy, writers distinguished between the educated and propertied public and the landless and feckless mob.

When we talk of 'the public interest' we often refer to the concerns of a particular polity; Immanuel Kant, however, argued that we only make 'public' use of our reason when we transcend the 'private' demands of civic and national institutions. Implicit in Kant's remarks on Enlightenment is a distinction between the public and the private in which the state is a *private* institution, a notion that upsets almost all other taxonomies of the public and the private. Such is the tangle of even the most obvious meanings that the compilers of the Oxford English Dictionary have been moved to admit that 'the varieties of sense are numerous and pass into each other by many intermediate shades of meaning . . . in some expressions more than one sense is vaguely present'.[10]

At a moment when our grasp of the concept of the public has become so confused, paradoxes multiply and compound the confusion. The publics that do exist as sites of effective and self-conscious decision about the future of our countries for the most part deliberate without publicity. Ours is an age of secluded, even secretive, publics. The active citizenship advocated by classical republicans does not venture into the daylight of general recognition.

A history of the public, even a brief history, will help us to distinguish between these varieties of sense. The intention is not to provide an exhaustive account of the ways in which we have used the word 'public' – such a thing would be all but indistinguishable from a history of the modern world. Rather, I want to explore the ideas surrounding the word that continue to inform our efforts to think and act politically. In this I have tended to concentrate on British and US notions. It is impossible to discuss British conditions sensibly without reference to the United States. In part because America has dominated the British political imagination for a generation; in part because America is itself a conscious attempt to re-imagine and improve upon Britain.

American readers who can forgive a British writer for padding about in their history will, I hope, gain something from what is, among other things, an attempt to reinvigorate the public life of the Republic. Readers elsewhere will be used to Anglo-American parochialism by now, but the ideas and assumptions of the English-speaking world continue to have an uncomfortable degree of influence worldwide. The so-called Washington Consensus drew extensively on British liberalism's notions of the public and the private spheres and on a highly tendentious reading of Britain and American economic development.[11] An historical sketch of Britain and the United States might provide something useful to those in other countries who are struggling to resist and reverse the madcap progress of Anglo-Saxon capitalism.

Secondly, the book describes how current ideas of the public and the private and of the division between them have contributed to a more general crisis in Anglo-American culture. Public communication has broken down to the point where we lack the means to establish an accurate account of the world as the basis for common deliberation. This breakdown is most obvious in the near-universal acceptance of the fantasy that an unrestrained private economy could be relied on as the provider of public goods. But it can be seen too in the state and the corporation's efforts to shape personality, culture and opinion, and in the way private categories – character and competence – dominate the description of politics.[12]

States and profit-driven institutions downplay or ignore those aspects of reality that undermine their authority. And when omission will not suffice, specialists are on hand to promote falsehoods in the service of a higher truth to which they claim to enjoy privileged access. Far from providing the general population with the information it needs if it is to conduct itself as a public, the major media groups and the institutions of the state endeavour to create a public opinion that amplifies, or least does not challenge, their own power. With this in view, the book explores the media's record in describing the economy in the long run-up to the financial crisis that began in 2007 and in the coverage of the period directly before the invasion of Iraq. In both cases I want to show how far removed from observable reality mainstream media accounts became.

Opinion-poll results that confirm the prevailing orthodoxy metastasize through the sources of general information; those that do not barely register. The levels of popular support for candidates and elected representatives feature heavily in news coverage. Popular interest in UFOs and 'conspiracy theories' also crops up regularly. Distrust of politicians, big business and the media in the United States and opposition to the privatization of state-run services in Britain do not. Media coverage of demonstrations against war or corporate globalization ignores the public contents of the demonstrators' arguments and focuses instead on their private motivations, or else on the forces that are secretly manipulating them. The population that emerges from the sum of these descriptions sometimes seems fearful and paranoid, sometimes responsible and civic-minded. But it rarely opposes those things that responsible elites consider to be inevitable.

The description of human nature that the general system of information provides denies us a properly human identity. And, in the absence of a public space in which we can engage with one another in an attempt to discover and secure the common good, we fall back on private strategies to shore up both our material conditions and our sense of self. We try to tailor our personalities to become more competitive. We manage our moods and adjust our attitudes through a process of self-surveillance and voluntary intoxication that in its reach and effectiveness far exceeds the achievements of totalitarian government. Or we seek chemical oblivion, sudden enrichment through gambling or the narcosis of being well-known in conditions of deepening distress. Our energetic, even frenzied, preoccupation with the private self plays out as a civic listlessness. And even as the need to collaborate in the production of public goods grows ever more acute, the economy consigns an ever greater number of us to enforced idleness.

Our inability to understand the world contributes to a deep dissatisfaction with our place in it. We lack the information we need to make sense of our predicament because such information is of no benefit to those who currently preside over the institutions on which we depend for information. And if this incomprehension causes an epidemic of destructive behaviour and despair in Anglo-America, it makes possible disaster worldwide, in so far as we fail to grasp how the governing powers use our money to pursue their interests. Solipsism at home makes possible state criminality abroad.

This is not meant to imply that it is impossible for the individual to develop a reasonably accurate sense of the world. In both Britain and the US lively alternative media have established themselves. In the United States, National Public Radio offers a platform for voices normally marginalized or ignored by the major broadcasters while a host of websites offer analysis from outside the pale of responsible opinion found in the mainstream. In Britain the liberal broadsheet press grants at least some publicity to critics of the prevailing order and, again, the web has allowed all shades of opinion a platform. But the alternative media remain chronically underfunded and, even when the more critical elements in the mainstream are taken into account, they reach only a small percentage of the population with any degree of regularity. The news and analysis that most people rely on comes folded with other products of the entertainment industry that corroborate and subsidize the view of the world they promote. More than this, the effort to understand the world comes at a considerable cost when an even tolerably accurate account contrasts so starkly with the vast bulk of widely accepted descriptions. Most people perhaps can appreciate that something has gone badly wrong but can see no benefit in the alienating work of figuring out exactly what, and what to do about it.

The third and final part of the book sets out a response to the failings in our systems of information that seems to me to be a precondition for both full economic recovery and substantive democracy. This response begins with quite modest proposals for changes in the ways in which the British and US media are funded. Whether citizens engage in the process or not, there is going to be a major shift in the way that the media in both countries are structured. The business model of terrestrial television is already under pressure while print publishing is in disarray. But so far most suggestions for reform do not address the cause of the media's inability to describe the world accurately – the domination of the commissioning process, and hence of the field of general description, by the employees of state and corporate institutions. Unreformed state-owned ('public service') media can no more adequately serve the public than commercial institutions can. Something else – what I call public commissioning – is necessary. The apparently minor changes I propose will enable us to create a gradually expanding space for public participation. Once we engage directly in the production of information in a shared institutional context we begin to develop the knowledge and the self-knowledge necessary to guide further political change. In becoming actors in the system of information we take the first step towards a more complete public identity. In other words, rather than presenting a set of vague general proposals for a transformation of the self and of society, I want to offer some concrete suggestions for how such a transformation might be made both possible and durable.

Whether one believes that only radical change to the structure of the economy can prevent massive ecological destruction, or that America must draw back from its efforts to build a world empire, only a reformed system of publicity can secure the levels of support necessary. Whether one wants to address the worst abuses of the current order or to secure a total transformation, everything flows from a reformed system of publicity. Only an adequately informed population, acting as a public, can legitimately decide how society is to be organized.

So, in outlining the first steps in a process of change to the structure of communications, and in making some suggestions as to how that process might develop, the book sketches the means by which the population as a whole can come to function as a public. Just as the shift from divinely mandated monarchy to a secular state governed by propertied men depended on changes in the economy of knowledge, and just as the current condominium of experts and investors depends on particular forms of state-corporate communications technology, a sovereign public requires a new constitution of information.

The book further outlines how, instead of providing an audience and an object of manipulation for the powerful, the population will become active in the commissioning of inquiry and then of action. It will no longer sit still waiting to be told what is necessary, but will deliberate and direct inquiry in the service of deliberation. The range of subjects that can reliably enter the general understanding will not be limited by the spectrum of opinion represented in Parliament, in Congress, or, most extensively, among the elites that control and populate the media and other powerful institutions. Instead, subjects will become obtrusive in the content of our conversations and of our political deliberation to the extent that the population demonstrates an appetite to know about them, and to the extent that the investigators commissioned can piece together an account that adds substance to our understanding. The state of affairs, rather than the range of admissible opinion, becomes the object of media interest, to the precise extent that the public is interested in discovering that state of affairs.

This process of public commissioning will have the effect of making more, and different, facts generally available. The state and the other large institutions that currently manage the media will no longer be responsible for creating public opinion (a responsibility they do not, and cannot, adequately discharge). The public itself will shape the news agenda and the wider information system by commissioning journalists and researchers. This new approach to journalism will enable all of us both to discover and to publicize information when our interests coincide with others'. More profoundly, the mechanisms for commissioning and assessing inquiry will establish local, regional and national publics.

The opening up of commissioning to general participation provides a model for the reform of science and technology. A new structure of information production will change our understanding of both current conditions and future possibilities. The monopoly power to define necessity enjoyed by the expert representatives of powerful institutions will be broken. Subjects that are currently riddled with enchantment and misunderstanding, from taxation, finance and the organization of private enterprise to the waging of war, will perhaps at last be clarified for the attention of a general public. At any rate, as the historical account in the earlier chapters will demonstrate, changes to the structure of information provision have far-reaching constitutional implications. Instead of the situation we have now, where the population is reconciled to the demands of the 'public interest' through the combined efforts of journalists, politicians and public relations experts, under the system I propose the general population secures the means to transform itself into a public.

The changes I propose will give us all the means to challenge untruth and to develop an accurate general understanding. They will also give us the means to recognize and defeat illegitimate power, since tyranny must depend at last on claims that are untrue. If our present arrangements seem justifiable to an informed public, then by all means leave them as they are. If, on the other hand, they seem unjustifiable in the light of a general understanding, they ought to be changed in ways that seem reasonable to the majority.

For myself, I believe that the current order of things depends on our accepting the comforts of an hallucinatory system of descriptions and a chain of pretended necessities that is only plausible in the absence of accurate information. This current order can only last as long as we remain unable to constitute ourselves as publics. Our rulers steered us into an economic crisis while those whose job it was to stay tolerably well acquainted with the facts of the world for the most part assured us that all was well. It is time to set aside the bleak lyricism of critical complaint and think practically about how we might alter the regime of truth in which we make our lives. By changing the institutional structures through which we generate and share information we begin to set ourselves free, since only a world more fully and more widely understood can be transformed. The first stage of this transformation, the clarification of general understanding, can only be resisted by the established powers on feeble and unconvincing pretexts. I am simply arguing that the population as a whole should secure access to the same power to inform itself that the powerful have always enjoyed.

These, then, are the aims of the book – to grab whatever seems useful from the last four centuries of Anglo-American history, to describe current conditions in the light of that history, and to set out a plan as to how we can make good on a long-held and long-frustrated hope: that we might live as humans, which is to say, in freedom.

PART 1

The Idea of the Public

CHAPTER ONE

The Classical Public

Every thinker puts some portion of the apparently stable world in peril.
John Dewey

T HOUGH THE VARIOUS ideas of the public that survive and overlap derive from particular historical moments they are also contemporary inventions. The tangle of meanings towards which the word now vaguely gestures holds most of us in permanent suspense, at some distance from the points of decision. If we can separate out those that contribute something to the composite sense of the word as it is used today, then some of the rubbish that stands in the way of effective political action will have been be cleared away.

In this regard, I am not so much an archaeologist as a grave robber, in the sense that my aim is not to reconstruct the past, but to take what strikes me as retaining some contemporary currency. For this reason Rome, rather than Greece or ancient Mesopotamia, seems like the natural starting point. For the republican form of government, which has won out over monarchy in much of the world, justified itself in terms of an attempt to renovate classical, and especially Roman, institutions. To be sure, the vague desire to emulate Rome lies close to the heart of the American state project. And if modern republicanism defines itself decisively against monarchy and the idea of power as a private possession, then it takes heart from the Roman traditions of regicide.

The Roman Republic was a *res publica*, a public possession. That is, it belonged to a community regulated by laws. A public in the Roman sense only exists when the state belongs to its citizens, when, as Cicero puts it, 'res publica [est] res populi'. Without ownership of the state, citizens cannot engage with one another as properly public actors. Freedom is only possible for those who have a share in state power; the subjects of a King can only ever be slaves. In practice only a tiny minority of Rome's inhabitants enjoyed full rights to participate in political life. Families with established claims to recognition – that is to say, the nobility – dominated political office and sought constantly to maintain and enhance the rights of their family to a share in the burdens and rewards of administration. Though talented outsiders could reach the ranks of the elite, nobility – the celebrity of virtue that justified claims to a fully public status – was more often inherited.

Rome was an aristocratic Republic – generation after generation a small number of families dominated public life. The heads of these families were intensely conscious of their obligation to maintain the family's glory and they would often claim pre-Republican and even divine origins to enhance their claim to public status. Each family was a monarchy in miniature and its claim to sovereign control of its own affairs could easily mutate into attempts to subvert the Republic for private glory. Furthermore public status depended on the authority that came from the disciplined control of the private household. The scandal of domestic disorder constantly threatened to cripple the public authority of a Roman noble.

At the same time the Roman Republic was characterized by an anxious insistence that the private world of the family and its obligations could be distinguished from the public world of the state. Rome's historians endlessly repeat the message that the closest private ties meant nothing when compared with the citizen's public duties. The consul Titus Manlius Torquatus executed his own son for engaging with the enemy in defiance of his father's orders; Lucius Junius Brutus went one better and had two of his sons killed for treason.

The Roman patriarch was always pushing at the limits of his private power. As the head of a family he had enormous powers of compulsion and when he went into the city to dispute and build alliances with other heads of family he accepted only those restrictions that could be effectively enforced. In one improving anecdote a consul forces his father, Fabius Maximus Cunctator, to dismount before approaching him. The hero of the war against Hannibal then assured his son that he meant no disrespect but that he considered 'publicly established laws to be more important than private obligations'.[1] While the story repeats the official dogma that duty to the state outweighs filial piety, it shows too that the prerogatives of a head of family could only be restrained by the vigorous exercise of lawful authority.

As long as the Republic survived, its ruling families insisted on a sharp distinction between the public, which is to say Rome, and the private, which is to say the family. Their energetic mutual surveillance took place in a culture where the control of the state was both the highest human excellence and the only truly honourable means to secure a fortune. Collectively, aristocrats worked to resist what they craved as individuals – the permanent ascendancy of one patriarch over all rivals. When Augustus, the founder of the first imperial dynasty, allowed the Senate to confer on him the title *Pater Patriae*, Father of the Fatherland, the significance was clear. Where once the whole Senate had styled themselves *patres*, from now on there was to be only one parent. The Republic had been finally subordinated to a single head of household, and as it became a private possession it became an empire. After Augustus aristocratic competitors for office no longer assert their right to public status, or secure it through popular recognition of their claims. Men enjoy the public status conferred on them by a monarch. In Europe the notion that a fully political identity is achieved through one's own exertions revives only when republicanism emerges to challenge monarchy many centuries later.

The word public was first used in early modern England to describe servants of the Crown. The idea of a public of office-holders became current in Tudor England, as did the notion that the country might be understood as a crowned Republic. Those who held office and served the monarch were public persons. The rest of the population was to busy itself with private matters.[2] But the legitimacy of this public of officer-holders rested on its claims to pursue the interests of the nation as a whole, to secure what the sixteenth-century administrator and philologist Sir Thomas Elyot called the 'public weal'. Public persons were public because the monarch appointed them, but they, like the King, served a public interest that encompassed more than their own interests. These early modern ideas of the public – the notion that public status derived from appointment by the state, and the notion that those who enjoyed this status held it in virtue of their service to the nation as a whole – have proved extremely durable. Together they inform a tradition that identifies the public interest and the national interest and insists on the right of a properly constituted state to promote them both.

During the English Civil War era, however, there is an important shift in the idea of the public as it operates in English political culture. Those who sought the establishment of an English Republic, including James Harrington and John Milton, insisted that all who were capable of citizenship should constitute the political nation. Public status did not derive from monarchical appointment, but from qualities possessed by individuals and from the exercise of those qualities in government. The political nation was understood as a 'body politic' of which each citizen was a constituent part. The example set by the free states of ancient Greece and Rome inspired the English republicans, and, according to Thomas Hobbes, led them astray. Writing in the 1690s Hobbes was to denounce the universities as 'the core of the rebellion' against Charles I, while his friend John Aubrey put John Milton's hostility to monarchy down to 'his being so conversant in Livy and the Roman authors, and the greatness he saw done by the Roman commonwealth, and the virtue of their great Commanders'.[3]

The argument between King and Parliament had long turned on the origins of political power. The Royalists insisted that power was the King's god-given possession and that the people were to be understood as subjects of an indivisible and divinely mandated power. On the day of his execution King Charles I rejected Roman notions and insisted that freedom 'consists in having of Government, those laws by which their life and their goods may be most their own. It is not for having share in Government, Sir, that is nothing pertaining to them. A subject and a sovereign are clean different things.'[4] The Parliamentarian Henry Parker asserted on the contrary that the people were 'the fountain and efficient cause' of secular power. Even kingly authority depended on popular consent. After all, as Parker pointed out, 'the Venetians and such other free nations' are 'so extremely jealous over their Princes . . . for fear of their bondage, that their Princes will dote upon their own wills and despise public councils and Laws'.[5]

The public that will both constitute and stand guard over the state is most fully developed in the writings of James Harrington. Following Cicero, Harrington argued in *The Commonwealth of Oceana* that citizens could only be truly free in a state when they together determine the content of its policies, that is, when the state was a public possession. Freedom in a free state meant more than the absence of active constraint, in the sense of freedom from fear of arbitrary arrest and confiscation. Free men are free because together they constitute the sovereign body of a state that in turn enacts their collective will. This collective power means that they do not have to rely on the goodwill of a prince. And it is in their union as deliberating citizens that a collection of private individuals achieves the status of a public. In Harrington's words 'the people taken apart are but so many private interests, but if you take them together they are the public interest'.[6]

When citizens do not hold power in this sense – when they do not together constitute the public and so together determine the public interest – they cannot be free, since in any other form of government they find themselves in a condition of dependence on a prince or on some combination of magnates. And to be in a state of dependence is to be a slave since, as Algernon Sidney put it, 'liberty solely consists in an independency upon the will of another'.[7] A slave might have a benevolent master, might in practice be able to live *as though* he were free, but he is still a slave and is as such prone to all the vices of servility. The English republicans drew heavily on Sallust's account of the collapse of Republican virtue. Sallust's Catiline prefigures Milton's Satan when he gives expression to a rhetoric of outraged competence:

> Ever since the Republic became the possession of a few great men it is they that have secured all the benefits of power – all taxes and tributes flow to them. The rest of us, for all that we are energetic and decent, nobles and commons alike, have become a mob without dignity or power. We are vulnerable [*obnoxii*] to those who should by rights fear us.[8]

Fear of injury is only one of the dangers in a state where effective power is a private possession. Under a despot men may be free from the fear of punishment while being enslaved by the prospect of rewards. The courtier represents for the republican imagination the spectacle of a man corrupted not so much by fear as by hope. If power is not in public hands then falsehood multiplies and virtue is impossible. The powerless compete to tell the powerful what they want to hear, while the powerful move to suppress the civic virtues that would threaten their control of the state. The Romans hated kings precisely because they were seen as a threat to individual excellence in others.[9] The republican ideal held out the prospect of a political settlement that was safe for individual virtue and honest speech. Where power is the private possession of a few men or of a prince, candid description menaces the system of power by undermining the lies used to make what is unjust seem justifiable, when deception of the people provides a career for the ambitious. Where the citizens share power, the truth can be acknowledged.

In a free state a citizen can rely only on himself and his fellow citizens to preserve the conditions of freedom and to resist the drift towards dependence and slavery. Mutual surveillance and constant exertion to prevent the capture of the state by private interests do not provide a guarantee of freedom. Vigilance bordering on neurotic suspicion would be the natural condition of a Republic of citizens. But the insistence that citizens should take responsibility for their own freedom, rather than relying on the restraint of their rulers, is a distinctive quality of republican thought.

English republicans did not necessarily think most of the population were capable of sharing power and therefore of being free. Many thought, or simply assumed, that women were incapable of citizenship as were those men who, through lack of property, existed in a state of dependence. Indeed in some strains of republican thought the claim to a public status enjoyed by property-owning males depended on the effective subordination of women, children and inferior males. In this they drew on pre-revolutionary traditions that had associated political authority with those who could both manage their own households and 'live idly and without manual labour'.[10]

Hence, while John Lilburne – whose doctrine of 'freeborn rights' continues to influence constitutional liberalism, especially in the US – argued that 'the poorest that lives, hath as true a right to give a vote, as well as the richest and greatest',[11] others advocated government in which 'an elite few governed in the interests of the whole commonwealth'.[12] Republicanism could be consistent with support for limited monarchy, meritocratic oligarchy (in the sense of rule by 'godly' men, for example), as well as democracy. But whatever limits to participation seemed natural in the seventeenth century we should not miss the fundamental point: liberty is not something that one is given, it is something that one achieves.

The republican ideal of freedom differs from the modern notion of liberal democracy in fundamental and troubling ways. The English republicans explicitly linked economic independence and political liberty. Without independent means of subsistence they believed that men would be driven into a state of dependence that would radically undermine their claims to be free. In Harrington's laconic formula 'he who wants bread is his servant that will feed him'.[13] And subsistence was not enough. For Harrington something like 'equality of estate' was needed in a free state. Indeed the distribution of land – of productive resources we would say now – determined the form of government. If one man owned the land, then absolute monarchy followed. If a few men controlled the land there would be mixed monarchy. Only if the 'whole people'[14] were landlords could a state hope to be a public possession: 'where there is inequality of estates, there must be inequality of power, and where there is inequality of power, there can be no commonwealth'.[15] Accordingly, Harrington, again drawing on his understanding of Rome's example, called for an agrarian law to limit the size of estates. In *The Commonwealth of Oceana* he writes:

> An equal agrarian is a perpetual law, establishing and preserving the balance of dominion by such a distribution, that no man or number of men, within the compass of the few or aristocracy, can come to overpower the whole people by their possession in lands.[16]

In a state of economic dependence we stand in fear of sudden dispossession. More insidiously, we are liable to be captured by the hope of arbitrary rewards and to alter our conduct and speech, even our beliefs, in order to obtain advantage. Even our desire for independence drives us into an ever more slavishly dependent cast of mind.

The doctrines of a free state are disconcerting because they force us to consider who amongst us can claim to be free. Certainly it is wishful thinking to suppose that we are indifferent to the threats and promises of our employers. We are obnoxious in the classical sense that we are vulnerable to the will of another. And it is still true that men who 'slide into a blind dependence upon one who has wealth and power' eventually 'care not what injustice they do, if they may be rewarded'.[17] An energetic and ambitious minority will plunge into an ever more abject submission to the institutional logic in which they find themselves, profiting from an illegitimate power to the extent that they come to embody it.

For at present such power and prestige as we enjoy usually depends on our, permanently insecure, footing in some bureaucratic, often corporate, hierarchy. As C. Wright Mills noted in the 1950s, 'to be celebrated, to be wealthy, to have power requires access to major institutions, for the institutional positions men occupy determine in large part their chance to have and to hold these valued experiences'.[18] When large, hierarchical institutions all but monopolize access to the goods we value and distribute them very unevenly they are apt to breed the vices of the court.

The republican model of government presents another reason for contemporary disquiet. In establishing the conditions of independence Harrington focused on the need for material subsistence, but in a vastly larger and more complex industrial society accurate information has become ever more crucial to those who aspire to public status. Where day-to-day experience and conversation once furnished men with the knowledge required for them to understand the world, we now rely on an extended infrastructure of reporting and research to remain in touch with the ever more remote world of effective decision-making. Yet we do not together monitor, let alone control, the means by which we become informed about matters beyond our immediate experience; nor is the network of descriptions on which we rely open to critical challenge from an engaged public. The media constantly tell us that we are individually autonomous and collectively sovereign. The same media have the power to ensure that we are neither. We depend on institutions we do not govern or understand in our efforts to understand and govern the wider world.

From the outset soothing voices could be heard, insisting that the notion of the Republic was impractical, excessive and unrealistic. William Paley, for example, assured his readers that 'those definitions ought to be rejected, which by making that essential to civil freedom which is unattainable in experience, inflame expectations that can never be gratified, and disturb the public content with complaints'.[19] The bleak theorist of the omnipotent state, Thomas Hobbes, also scorned the idea of the Republic and the world of Roman virtue it both promised and demanded. As far as Hobbes was concerned the state could take whatever form it liked. It could call itself a civic Republic or a despotism on the Turkish model. The state was not constituted by an individual chosen by God or by natural persons arranged as a public. The state was an artificial animal, entirely self-sufficient and self-justifying. And the substance of the state was everywhere the same, it was absolute power, a permanent capacity to daunt all rivals, a frozen violence holding all subordinate powers in a condition of enforced peace. The state was the sole public institution but it did not rely on the consent of any existing public for its legitimacy. Necessity provided all the legitimacy needed since without states man would find himself in the chaos of war that was his natural condition.

According to Hobbes this was the reality that the republicans, drunk on classical learning, failed to grasp. Individual freedom amounted to no more than being left alone to pursue one's own lawful projects under the state's watchful eye. Any other concept of freedom was wishful thinking. In a much-quoted passage Hobbes mocks the citizens of Lucca and their republican pretensions:

The Athenians, and Romans were free; that is, free commonwealths: not that any particular men had the liberty to resist their own representative; but that their representative had the liberty to resist, or invade other people. There is written on the turrets of the city of Lucca in great characters at this day, the word LIBERTAS; yet no man can thence infer, that a particular man has more liberty, or immunity from the service of the commonwealth there, than in Constantinople. Whether a commonwealth be monarchical, or popular, the freedom is still the same.[20]

Harrington returns this contempt for the free state with interest. Commenting on Hobbes's view that the liberty of a commonwealth is not the liberty of particular men within it, Harrington retorts that

he might as well have said that the estates of particular men in a commonwealth are not the riches of particular men, but the riches of the commonwealth; for equality of estates causes equality of power, and equality of power is the liberty, not only of the commonwealth, but of every man.[21]

Furthermore, insists Harrington, it is one thing to claim that a citizen of Lucca has no more liberty *from* the law than a Turk and quite another to claim that he has no more liberty *by* the law:

The first may be said of all governments alike; the second scarce of any two; much less of these, seeing it is known that, whereas the greatest Bashaw is a tenant, as well of his head as of his estate, at the will of his lord, the meanest Lucchese that has land is a freeholder of both, and not to be controlled but by the law, and that framed by every private man to no other end (or they may thank themselves) than to protect the liberty of every private man, which by that means comes to be the liberty of the commonwealth.[22]

In the twentieth century Isaiah Berlin influentially restated Hobbes' rejection of the idea that true liberty was only to be found where citizens organized as a public controlled the state. In *Two*

Concepts of Liberty Berlin described positive and negative liberty in terms that decisively favoured what Noel Annan called, in a revealing moment of amnesia, 'the classic English interpretation of liberty' – that to be free is to be left unmolested by arbitrary power. This is 'the classic English interpretation of liberty' only in the sense that it is what remains once the many advocates of an English Republic are removed from view.

Berlin describes negative freedom in ways that would be familiar to Hobbes, indeed he quotes Hobbes in a footnote: 'A free man . . . is he that . . . is not hindered to do what he has a will to.' It follows for Berlin that 'a frontier must be drawn between the area of private life and that of public authority'.[23] Freedom is something that is enjoyed in private, not something that is exercised in public. Berlin, like Hobbes, deals with the republican conception of virtue by ignoring its key arguments. Individuals are free when they are unmolested by the state. When they are dependent on others for survival Berlin cannot see that they are unfree, since they are free to defy their betters and starve.

Berlin's elaborates his case against positive liberty in a way that is, at best, eccentric. He begins sensibly enough:

> The 'positive' sense of the word 'liberty' derives from the wish on the part of the individual to be his own master. I wish my life and decisions to depend on myself, not on external forces of whatever kind. I wish to be the instrument of my own, not other men's, acts of will. I wish to be a subject, not an object. . .[24]

He goes on to point out that positive liberty of this self-actualizing kind has sometimes turned into a blind faith in some abstract entity that realizes the true perfection of the imperfect human individual – the State, the Party, Reason, History, Human Nature. In the name of this abstraction the advocates of positive freedom can then coerce their fellows, secure in the knowledge that they are helping them to become truly free. Hence the Bolsheviks developed their enthusiasm for education and, especially, re-education and accepted the need to exterminate those social elements that incorrigibly stood in the way of the general freedom. Having discovered the nature of true freedom, Soviet communists were confident that they were justified in coercing those who opposed them.

But Berlin disastrously confuses the drive for effective autonomy with the desire to dominate others by allowing one possible development – or more accurately, one perversion – of positive liberty to stand for the concept as a whole. Berlin is thus able to conclude that those who seek to defend the freedom of the individual from external compulsion are 'almost at the opposite pole' from those who believe in positive liberty: 'The former want to limit authority as such. The latter want it placed in their own hands.'[25] This is suavely effective rhetoric but it allows Berlin to ignore centuries of republican practice as well as the substance of republican theory in the English tradition. The point for republicans is that 'authority as such' can only be limited effectively when a public of citizens is its sole source.

Berlin argued, for reasons that are essentially vapid, that the positive freedom to engage in the political process would inevitably conflict with the individual's sphere of private immunity. But positive liberty, in the sense of freedom to engage in the formation and conduct of the state, does not entail any of the extravagances that he ascribes to it. The desire to be Somebody does not necessarily decay into the worship of Something.

Berlin is right to point out that democracies can sometimes act in illiberal ways. But he is wrong to claim that people can be free when they do not have the power to control and direct the state. Wrong too to imagine that people can be free when they cannot be confident in their material independence. Without secure access to the means of subsistence they will not be able to assert themselves fearlessly as citizens. Without political power they cannot defend the independence they have. And while the citizens of a Republic may never be invulnerable to the antics of an activist state, they will surely be more secure than those who must rely on the restraint and good manners of their rulers. To repeat, liberty in the republican sense of the word requires more than freedom from active coercion. It requires also the power to shape the state, and to do so from a position of material independence. A citizen who fears she may lose her livelihood if she speaks out is not meaningfully free unless she is a hero or a fool.

Perhaps Berlin's distrust of positive liberty derives from his conviction that the population organized as a public cannot set limits to its own power. We are, according to this view, unable to discern and protect our private interests through public deliberation. Certainly the language of true liberty had been mightily abused in the decades before Berlin wrote in praise of negative liberty. But what Berlin sees as liberty is not liberty truly stated. The enjoyment of private property and the unmolested experience of life in a network of private relationships do not suffice as conditions for freedom. Without a public identity we are not free, any more than a free-range chicken is free. Indeed, though we may count ourselves lucky, and develop all manner of private properties of mind, we are not, in one sense, even fully human.

While Hobbes and his intellectual heirs denounced the English republicans for demanding too much, they were also attacked for demanding too little. Gerard Winstanley set out what he saw as the conditions of true liberty in *The Law of Freedom*. In the opening sections he sketches out the various ways of construing freedom. Freedom of trade, he says, is no more than 'freedom under the will of a conqueror' if it is conducted under the existing distribution of property. Freedom of religion would be an unsettled freedom, that is, men would have no security when they sought to assert their religious freedom. Sexual freedom was no more than the freedom of 'wanton, unreasonable beasts'. And what of those who claim that 'it is true freedom that the elder brother shall be landlord of the earth, and the younger brother a servant'?[26]

This is 'but a half freedom', says Winstanley, and one 'that begets murmurings, wars and quarrels'. Winstanley believed that there could be no just basis for great inequalities of wealth and power. Rich men depend on the work of other men for their wealth: 'if a man have no help from his neighbour, he shall never gather an estate of hundreds and thousands a year'. Great concentrations of wealth depend on capturing the value created by others. There had to be some trickery involved, thought Winstanley. The plain-hearted poor end up working for the idle rich only through the exercise of 'covetous wit'. The pretensions of the propertied gentleman were no more than the swagger of a successful fraudster. At a time when covetous wit has brought vast wealth to a tiny number of knowledgeable operators and the prevailing descriptions have recast their work of upward distribution as a kind of productive labour, the contemporary implications must surely be obvious. True freedom could only be had, thought Winstanley, when men had equal, and equally secure, access to the means of subsistence, the land itself. 'True Commonwealth's freedom', he declared, 'lies in the free enjoyment of the earth.'[27]

If everyone could live independently then men could cooperate freely for their mutual advantage. Only then could men speak plainly to one another, without the fear that they would lose favour, livelihood, or life. A nation where only 'older brothers', the property-holding heads of households, were free would only be half free. Freedom required material independence as well as the formal enjoyment of rights and the absence of active coercion by the state or anyone else. Reluctantly or not, many of the republicans concluded that only a minority could therefore be free. Winstanley, on the contrary, decided that all must therefore become independent in order that all might be free. In the gap between those who sought a Republic built on a Roman conception of virtue and those, like

Winstanley, who thought that to be human warranted liberation, we begin to see the shape of what haunts this book, the outline of a public that is at once sovereign and universal.

The older brothers of Cromwell's Republic and the plain-hearted poor could not find common cause once the King had been defeated. In the century that followed the yeomen who had supplied the Parliamentary armies with their cavalry and the republicans with their constituency were driven into conditions of dependency as the great estates expanded. The poor, far from enjoying the common treasury of the earth, lost what common rights they had in a wave of enclosures. The magnates, who were terrified of radical democracy and could see no great protection from it in a Republic, instead brought back monarchy. An aristocracy that preferred order and the secure possession of private property to republican virtue installed first Charles II and then William III to be their King. The Bill of Rights, which set out the terms on which Parliament accepted William III, avoided the language of republicanism, and the successful conspirators in Parliament spoke instead of 'asserting their ancient rights and liberties'.[28]

English republicanism provided an important resource for the framers of the United States constitution, but key principles have all but vanished from the openly stated political culture of both Britain and America, most notably the insistence that only a rough 'equality of estate' can substantiate the formal equality of voting citizens. To the economic equality advocated by Harrington and others we must, however, add equality of information. Otherwise we will face steady dispossession by those who combine restless ambition with a talent for fraud.

CHAPTER TWO

Private Vices and Public Virtues

T HE REPUBLICAN MODEL did not establish itself in Britain
as its advocates had hoped. Monarchy was restored, albeit on
ambiguous terms. William III insisted on his ancient prerogatives and
Parliament accepted his demands. The monarchy's control of policy
weakened only gradually, since it was possible for both William and
the Hanoverian Kings to use foreign funds to coordinate support
from the political elite. But an activist King would not challenge the
system established in 1688 and seek to rule in defiance of Parliament.
The popular charisma of the monarchy declined. Where the Stuarts
had been able to call on a national constituency – and would continue
to do so in parts of Britain well into the eighteenth century – the
dynasties that replaced them had no desire to establish themselves in
the hearts of their subjects. Such bonds were dangerous. Better that
the King remain a distant figure of duty and tradition than that he
become a figure promising a change in conditions.

The bulk of the population were offered a fantasy of unbroken
tradition and time-honoured obedience to the ancestral order. The
English came to see themselves as a private people, secure in the
enjoyment of their God-given freedom, happiest at home, or making
themselves at home in someone else's country. They were encouraged to be ignorant, and proud, of their governing institutions. The
philosopher David Hume later argued that even those few who could
see through the 'prejudices in favour of birth and family' would
want to preserve them in everyone else in order to maintain 'a due

subordination in society'.[1] Meanwhile, the political class governed in its own interests and acted to ensure that the sum of its private concerns was understood to constitute the public or the national interest.

These oligarchs had no desire to reveal the reality of power in Britain, since to do so might risk awakening memories of the Republic. Better the ancestral constitution in theory and an oligarchy in fact than a system open to scrutiny and a people enlivened by the prospect of radical or apocalyptic change. More than a century after the Civil War observers saw in expressions of mob violence the spectre of the Republic. Edward Gibbon wrote of the Gordon Riots in June 1780 that 'forty thousand puritans such as they might be in the time of Cromwell have started out of their graves'.[2] As long as the Kings accepted the limits of their power relative to the propertied classes, monarchy and aristocracy were safe in the shared space of a constitutional fiction. Political life in England took on the quality of a paradox. From now on what was public was to be clothed in secrecy and deceit. Participation in government was to be tightly restricted and conducted on terms that were not generally explained. Those who determined state policy did so as loyal servants of a monarchy that they themselves had installed.

The effectual political nation – the successors to the 'public men' of the Tudor and Stuart monarchy – that emerges in England after 1688 was tiny: Henry Fielding famously said that a 'nobody' was 'all the people in Great Britain, except about 1200'. But this ruling elite owed more to the republican tradition than its propagandists through the ages would want to admit. The magnates that brought William and Mary to the throne and negotiated the terms on which they would govern appreciated that their own freedom depended on their participation in the political sphere. Rather than contenting themselves with 'negative' freedom, they secured positive control of revenues and legislation. They tacitly held in reserve the ultimate power, to remove one King and put another in his place. The oligarchy organized in Parliament did not wish to be left in peace, to pursue their private concerns and to enjoy their private property. Freedom from state interference was not enough. Instead they engaged with the state both to protect and to promote their interests. The popular language of liberty elaborated in the eighteenth century, and the social egalitarianism that famously accompanied it, was something of a cover for an active ruling class that used its control of legislature to deliver the policies it desired. The burden of taxation fell on consumption and successive acts of enclosure further consolidated aristocratic power at the expense of small and middling independent farmers.

As noted, this effectually governing public justified itself at first through appeals to the ancient constitution. There was no trace in the Bill of Rights of the idea that the people were the 'fountain and efficient cause' of power. But a comprehending public was now in effective control of the state. It was much more narrowly circumscribed than many republicans had hoped, and in place of Roman candour it spoke with carefully organized hypocrisy. But it was the political nation, and its common concerns constituted the animating principles of state power. Hence those who had planned the coup against James II could not resist justifying themselves retrospectively through an appeal to the idea of a contract between people and sovereign. After 1688 John Somers argued that James II had not simply left the throne vacant. He had broken the compact that existed between Crown and people and therefore lost his right to rule. What at the time had been all nervous improvisation became a vindication of the idea that Kings could not rule without a decent respect for the opinions of their subjects. John Locke's *Two Treatises of Government* provided an elegant vindication of the plotters of 1688. The first treatise put an end to the notion of divine right and the second established the necessity of consent from at least some of the governed if power was to be legitimate.

The ruling class that established itself after 1688, like all durably successful ruling classes, paid close attention to those outside its ranks. The clique that brought William III to Britain went on to create a faction within the Whig Party (the so-called 'junto') that acted as a link between the King and the financial powers in the City. And it wasn't only the merchant princes of the City that concerned the political classes. Locke's second *Treatise* reinforced the prerogatives of private property and established limits on those of the monarchy. But this weakening of monarchy in the interests of private property came at a price. The people would have to be taken into account, would indeed have to be granted public status of sorts, to the extent that they qualified in virtue of their private possessions.

This public was defined in various ways. The Earl of Shaftsbury thought that the public consisted of those that had 'seen the World and informed themselves of the Manners and Customs of the several Nations of Europe'.[3] This disqualified most men and nearly all women, but still included more people than sat in Parliament. A more expansive, and less exalted, notion of the public can be detected in the decision to establish a national museum 'not only for the inspection and entertainment of the learned and the curious, but for the general use and benefit of the public'.[4] This public went to the theatre, read the newspapers and supported the settlement of 1688.

As long as the majority of the population could be kept at arm's length from decision-making there was no harm in the idea of a contractual state. Indeed if the King based his authority on the consent of the governed, the state derived important benefits; the King borrowed money on behalf of the nation, rather than as a steroidal aristocrat acting on his own account, and so the nation stood behind the debt. The historian Sidney Homer notes that 'by the 1720s the English national credit could be effectively pledged behind the loans of government in the manner of the mediaeval Italian republics, the provinces of seventeenth century Holland, and modern democracies'.[5] Rule by consent of the propertied enabled Britain to establish a national system of credit.

At any event, though the public in the sense of the political nation properly defined remained quite small, and certainly smaller than many Civil War republicans had hoped, the scene was set for a new articulation of the idea of the public. In the early modern era the idea had referred to those who held office under the monarchy. The republicans had offered a more expansive notion, where the public, qualified by economic independence and virtue, collectively embodied the state. But in both cases there was no sense that the public might exist outside the state. The republicans looked to a future where all persons capable of independent thought and virtuous action participated in government and together articulated the public interest. They did not have in mind a public that would scrutinize and hold the state to account while remaining at a distance from its institutions. In this sense the republican public was somewhat like the monarchical public that it sought to replace.

But after the 1688 settlement something like modern public opinion, through which the actions of the state could be challenged, began to take shape. During the Civil War, literacy had spiked as a mass readership sought emancipation through the written word.[6] Radical ideas had reached vastly more readers than under the King. In 1640 just over 20 political pamphlets appeared. Two years later the number had risen to nearly two thousand.[7] The end of the Republic and the return of the monarchy reduced the scope for popular engagement in the political sphere. But a reading culture recovered, driven by energetic publishers who substituted entertainment for agitation, and displaced aristocratic patronage as they did so. This new culture industry, characterized by the novel rather than the pamphlet, supported, and was supported by, the metropolitan culture that developed in the period after the Restoration. Thousands of coffee-houses, each with their devoted clientele, scores of clubs, where men could meet in conditions of formal equality, and taverns, in which all kinds of people were wont to 'blend and jostle into harmony',[8] provided venues for sociability for writers and publishers, playwrights and poets, financiers and tradesmen as well as aristocrats and gentleman politicians. As early as the 1670s the authorities were complaining, in terms that will become familiar in the centuries that follow, that:

> Men have assumed to themselves a liberty, not only in coffee-houses but in other places and meetings, both public and private, to censure and defame the proceedings of the State, by speaking evil of things they understand not, and endeavouring to create and nourish an universal jealousy and dissatisfaction in the minds of His Majesties good subjects.[9]

As literacy once again expanded and commercial networks grew to satisfy popular appetites, writers came to see an anonymous 'public' of book-buyers as a viable source of patronage. And this new literary culture thought of itself as a 'commonwealth of polite letters'.[10] Letters to the editor of the *Spectator* were posted through the jaws of a lion fixed on the wall of a local coffee-house, Button's,[11] a larky reference to the Bocca di Leone in Venice, where the people could secretly post their suggestions and complaints to the governing authorities.

Jürgen Habermas situates the creation of what he calls the public sphere in London's new social promiscuity. A public of private individuals educated by both literary culture and the shared life of the city begins to discover itself as a group with shared values and a shared willingness to comment on matters of common concern. He notes that, by the end of the eighteenth century, the public, in the sense of a group outside of the state and Parliament to which politicians had finally to defer, certainly exists as a feature of aristocratic rhetoric. Here is Charles Fox, speaking in 1792:

> It is certainly right and prudent to consult public opinion . . . If the public opinion did not happen to square with mine; if, after pointing out to them the danger, they did not see it in the same

light with me, or if they considered that another remedy was preferable to mine, I should consider it my due to my king, due to my
Country, due to my honour to retire, that they might pursue the
plan which they thought better, by a fit instrument, that is by a
man who thought with them . . . but one thing is most clear, that I
ought to give the public the means of forming an opinion.[12]

The public in this sense becomes the spectral authority to which
challengers to the existing combination of King and clique can
appeal. The public was also the country and, as Habermas points out,
'the opposition, as the party of the country, always appeared to be in
the right versus the party of the court corrupted by "influence"'.[13]
Perhaps we see in Squire Western's complaints in *Tom Jones* about
'Hanover rats' a premonition of that staple of modern American
politics, the run against Washington. Certainly the emotional
resources of Whig and Tory rhetoric, as well as those of Victorian
liberalism and conservatism, find uncanny echoes in the brand associations of the Democrat and Republican parties.[14]

Habermas makes much of the increasingly public nature of
political life in Britain in the eighteenth century; after a series of
campaigns by John Wilkes the proceedings of Parliament are finally
made available to the reading public; individuals outside the elite
take an interest in state policy and draw on new publications for
information. Habermas argues that a public sphere emerges in
Britain that is the collective achievement of private actors. It is their
engagement with the cultural productions of the time, their experience in the new intimacy of the bourgeois household, and their
exertions in the market-place that give them the knowledge and
confidence to challenge the existing political classes. According to
Habermas they aspire to establish truth, rather than authority, as the
animating principle of legislation. This public sphere is propertied
and male, and its claims to universalism are always suspect, but as
a space for rational debate constructed by private individuals and

situated outside the state in Habermas's account it represents something profoundly new.

The idea of the public sphere as something like 'a discursive community of citizens . . . who are outside the state but who nonetheless deliberate, debate and otherwise express opinions about state policy' has become very influential in academia in the United States, especially in debates about media reform.[15] Efforts to improve journalism by addressing the profession's values and practices that go by the name of public journalism draw extensively on the concept. Edward Lambeth has written that 'were public journalism to require a philosophical patron saint, Habermas, arguably, would appear to be a logical candidate'.[16] In some ways this salience isn't surprising.

Habermas's historical account, where the prototypical public sphere emerges from the private actions of private men, appeals to advocates of public journalism since it appears compatible with an acceptance of the prevailing institutional order. If commercial institutions were able to create a vigorous and critical media culture in the late eighteenth century, then there is nothing to stop modern newspaper companies from doing the same. Advocates of public journalism exhort journalists to revive the public sphere and to enliven civil society – 'to form as well as inform the public' in Jay Rosen's formulation – while leaving both market forces and state power untouched. Reform of the media becomes a matter of journalists doing a better job. The formula appeals strongly to liberal self-love, but, as Michael Schudson points out, 'nothing in public journalism removes power from the journalists or the corporations they work for . . . always authority about what to write and whether to print stays with the professionals'.[17] The invocation of the public sphere dignifies journalism by suggesting that media reform can be achieved by a change of attitude by journalists. Habermas's public of private individuals seems to justify leaving the management of the media in the hands of private actors, whether they be individual employees or the companies they work for. In such circumstances calls for more extensive civic engagement by journalists can scarcely be distinguished from calls for more pervasive market research.[18]

Fox appeals to the public, even calls it into existence, to adjudicate between the claims of those who form the government and those who aspire to do so. The public, in the sense of a force outside of the state and the Parliament, takes substance from conflicts within the elite. Public opinion becomes in one sense paramount, inasmuch as the elites, once they have adopted Lockean ideas of a government based on the consent of the governed, cannot be seen to defy the judgement of the new public of sensibility. But this public is an arbiter in struggles at the centre, it does not develop policies and choose the executors of those policies, whatever Fox might sycophantically suggest. Rather it stands in judgement of men who are qualified to act in the political arena and it chooses between them. The educated public listens and observes, critically to be sure. But it does not speak for itself. It chooses between candidates offered in the electoral process, and can applaud or catcall the activities of the political performers. It can be delighted by charisma, by the poetry of the campaign, even by the content of a platform, but it is not expected to share in government. Though flattered with the title of public, the emerging society organized around the club, the tavern, the stage and the novel is better understood as an audience.

This audience was from the outset subject to every form of dramatic manipulation. The historian Edmund Morgan notes that as early as 1681 constituents were sending instructions to Parliament in which 'the similarity of the wording suggests not only that they were inspired from above but that they originated in a single source'. In the election of 1742 instructions from the constituencies helped swing the result, prompting the losers to complain that 'it is the People that speak but the Malecontents dictate. A gross piece of state Mummery, wherein A instructs B how B shall instruct A'.[19] This early example of what will later be called 'astroturfing' is part of a wider process in which the idea of the public is deployed to undermine or reinforce factions within the ruling class.

Habermas argues more persuasively that the image of the English public provides an inspiration for liberal movements throughout Europe. Certainly the critical culture that emerges in France and Germany in the later part of the eighteenth century and provides a venue where a programme of reform can be elaborated closely resembles his model of a public sphere as a public of private individuals. In the struggle against absolutism and ecclesiastical power, Britain had enormous charisma as a champion of liberty. But in Britain a public of private individuals never establishes itself as the consistent originator of political action. Decisions mostly remain in the hands of aristocratic elites that determine policy within an agreed framework of accommodation with the mercantile and financial interests and the Crown. The public is important for maintaining dynamic competition between the politicians, but while it is guided towards judgements about their competence and probity, it only very rarely determines what they do.[20]

Somewhat removed from the metropolitan world of aristocratic intrigue, David Hume and Adam Smith developed an account of political economy, and an accompanying account of the relationship between the public and the private, that achieves massive general authority not once but twice – first in the era of late Hanoverian and early Victorian *laissez-faire* and again in the generation just past. Hume and Smith both rejected the heroic ideal of active citizenship and insisted that men should, wherever possible, be left to pursue their own interests in whatever way they chose. The owners of property, acting as buyers and sellers, were best left to discover the price of goods. Efforts to intervene by political authority would be useless, if not downright harmful, and would anyway infringe on the right of the individual to dispose of his property as he wished. Canting statesmen could not be trusted to safeguard the public interest. The frankly selfish activities of individuals engaged in free exchange would do a far better job. After all, men strive to improve themselves in order, in Smith's words, 'to be observed, to be attended to, to be taken notice of with sympathy'.[21] The steady impulse to better our condition and our status makes it possible for men to live both freely and in a relative harmony with one another, even when those involved have not 'the least intention to serve the public'.[22]

There is in Hume and Smith a marked reluctance to rely on aristocratic virtue to secure the common interest, though they recognized the need to maintain the distinction between 'the elegant part of mankind' and those who were 'immersed in mere animal life'.[23] But while the Earl of Shaftsbury had claimed that 'to philosophize, in a just signification, is but to carry Good-Breeding a step higher',[24] Smith justified, to himself at any rate, the exclusion of most of the population from intellectual autonomy by an appeal to the division of labour: 'In opulent or commercial society, to think or reason comes to be, like every other employment, a particular business, which is carried on by a very few people, who furnish the public with all the thought and reason possessed by the vast multitudes that labour.'[25] The tiny minority who were able to reason had enormous political power, since, according to Hume, 'the governors have nothing to support them but opinion'.[26] A government wins a great deal of security if 'the generality of the state, or . . . those who have the force in their hands' tend to believe that 'the particular government which is established is equally advantageous with any other that could easily be settled'. This Hume calls the opinion of public interest. Added to it are the opinions of right to property and the opinion of right to power. Together these constitute the basis for stable government.[27] One can maintain the existing social order if one controls the opinions of those one governs. In the system of political economy described by Hume and Smith private impulses deliver public benefits; society can be at once dynamic and stable while people can enjoy both freedom – in the sense of non-interference – and opulence. But the preoccupations of commercial competition deprive most people of the leisure and resources to think independently and they instead must rely on others to form their opinions. In the market society of the eighteenth-century liberals, the provision of opinion is a trade like any other and the majority therefore lack an independent understanding of their condition. They may feel themselves free and they may be rich in fact, but they cannot reason for themselves. Their liberty remains a kind of license.

If the labouring multitudes depended on a particular business to furnish them with their thoughts, then those who controlled the production of opinion could control the state. From the outset the market-place of ideas favoured the wealthy and was subject to manipulation by powerful interests. Once advertising became an important source of revenue, the thought and reason of the labouring multitudes was made subject to the steady influence of the rich. In liberal political economy we can see the outlines of a modern public as a group furnished with opinions by others, granted public status by virtue of their acquiring the habits of thought and beliefs manufactured for their consumption.

The eighteenth-century state's respect for private property should not be understood as a simple limit on its power. The state would profit from the expansion of the private economy beyond the bounds of the household. It was hoped that freedom from arbitrary interference would encourage industry, reward individual initiative, and promote domestic order. Samuel Johnson's remark that 'there are few ways in which a man can be more innocently employed than in getting money' summed up the hope that the pursuit of wealth begat, if not virtue, then at least blameless immunity from politico-religious enthusiasm.[28] It was certainly the case that higher levels of economic activity increased tax receipts and generated a surplus that could be invested in the national debt. Britain's ability to fight a series of European wars in the eighteenth century while providing large subsidies to its allies derived in part from the massive expansion of the private economy.

The historian Ellen Meiskins Wood has argued that Locke's celebration of the public benefits of private property helped to legitimate
the expansion of English settlement in North America.[29] Unlike other
promoters of empire, Locke did not attempt to justify imperialism
at the level of the state. Rather, settlers were entitled to take possession of land when its current inhabitants were not improving it, or
rather when their failure to improve meant the land did not constitute property in the full sense. The English made American land
more profitable (calculated in English terms, of course) and so were
entitled to drive the natives from it, since insufficiently productive
land was a kind of waste. The English could not pretend that they
had found in America a *terra nullius*. But Locke assured them that
their efforts to improve the land and the integration of what they
produced into a market system justified them in exterminating what
Charles Dilke would later call the 'cheaper peoples' of the world. Not
surprisingly, those British and American intellectuals who sought to
renovate liberal ideas in the second half of the twentieth century did
so as part of an attempt to restore the dynamism of the state as a force
for defending the propertied at home and abroad. In both Margaret
Thatcher and Ronald Reagan we find the same combination of an
apparently sincere admiration for the independent man of property
and a sentimental and aggressive nationalism.

The ideas of the public that can be traced back to the period
after the Glorious Revolution are distinct from the monarchical and
republican ideas that precede them. The public is not a body of office-
holders dependent on the Crown for its status, nor is it an expanded
'body politic' of republican citizens. In one version the public is
external to the operations of the state and acts as a critical audience
for the activities of those who seek to determine policy. This public is
both literate and reasonable, yet it does not exercise political power
directly. It is permanently on guard against threats to liberty – above
all threats to the prerogatives of property, being enlisted in defence
of the existing, and steepening, inequalities of eighteenth-century

Britain. But this public of private individuals, bound together by ties of sociability and by the operations of a nascent culture industry, does not usually develop programmes of its own; in Isaiah Berlin's terminology it is more concerned with negative than with positive liberty.

In the liberal thought of Hume and Smith 'the public' all but vanishes as an entity distinct from the sum of economic actors. The 'public good' emerges from the decisions of individuals whose motives are purely private.[30] More vaguely, we find in the eighteenth century the origins of the public as a term of art – the public as a feature of elite rhetoric and an object of elite subterfuge. All the while an effectually governing group controls the state and uses it as a vehicle to serve its interests. In the din of liberty the rural population is impoverished while the City and the aristocracy, under cover of monarchy, make common cause. Here perhaps we see the paradox of modern power, the fact of a secret public.

Yet this does not exhaust the legacy of the period. In the work of Immanuel Kant we find a conception of the public that presents a much more serious challenge to the established order than is at first apparent. In his essay *What is Enlightenment?* Kant sets out to explain both what Enlightenment consists of and how it might be made compatible with a stable civil order. His description of Enlightenment itself is familiar now to the point of cliché. Enlightenment, he says, is 'the process of moving out of a self-incurred immaturity of mind . . . Dare to know, *aude sapere*, that is the watchword of Enlightenment.'[31] But his account of how such behaviour might be possible is much more exotic and much more important, and it turns on his distinction between the public and the private.

Kant argues that when we act in an institutional or social role, we do not and cannot exercise our reason with total or perfect rigour. It is only when we step outside these roles, where we spend much of lives, and in which we find much of what is valuable in them, that we can hope to reason in a manner that is unconstrained. For Kant the crucial distinction is between the public and the private use (*öffentlich gebrauch* and *Privatgebrauch*) of reason. He gives the example of a priest who can honourably fulfil his private duties as long as he is not sure that the dogmas of his faith are false. But when he considers faith in the light of reason he is free to state the ways in which he thinks these doctrines might be in error. Indeed as 'a scholar addressing a reading public' he is *obliged* to speak freely and so becomes the prototype of enlightened action. We can labour under any number of private restraints without retarding the progress of general Enlightenment, so long as the sphere of public reason remains free.

Kant's description of the entirety of our institutional and social life as a realm of private reason runs contrary to a more conventional schema in which the state is understood as a public realm while the family and the market-place are private. It also undermines the separation of a cadre of experts from an inexpert public that emerges in the eighteenth century and remains with us today. Experts who remain bound to institutional roles and interested constituencies cannot make public use of their reason – they are not, in Kant's sense of the word, enlightened. It follows that the extent to which individuals acting in their capacity as placeholders control general debate traces the remaining work of Enlightenment.

For Kant, everyone, to the extent that they can reason without limits and yet have limits imposed on them by the demands of society, is both a public and a private actor. The reasoning public was not a bourgeois audience that stood in judgement of the state. The state's officers, from the King down, are themselves private actors. But they are also potentially public actors, to the extent that they are capable of reasoning outside their institutional roles and of transcending the habits of thought that develop within these roles. Only in this way do individuals become capable of enlightened activity. And for Kant the discoveries of reason exercised publicly outweigh the demands of obedience. The public of enlightened exchange runs parallel with the private world of the state, the family and all other institutions. The personnel are the same but the modes of engagement differ profoundly.

Kant situates enlightened activity in a space separate from the ongoing world of institutional and personal commitments. It is a model of Enlightenment that stands in direct opposition to our own arrangements. At present, reliable access to publicity depends above all on institutional position. Individuals are invited to share their views and to contend with one another in debate to the extent that they can demonstrate some private stake in the matter at hand. There are occasional exceptions. Novelists, actors and entertainers sometimes speak out on matters outside their areas of immediate expertise in ways that reach an audience, with mixed results. Celebrity substitutes for institutional interest as grounds for being heard. Members of the public are aggregated in opinion polls whose terms they do not set and cannot challenge. Occasionally they appear in front of the camera, or are quoted in print, edited in ways they do not control. But for the most part, directly interested parties, acting in what Kant would call a private capacity, populate those discussions and debates that become widely known. In the current division of labour the views of individuals, in so far as they are freely reasoning beings, are 'private', they do not trouble the major systems of representation and indeed they are often kept secret by those working within powerful institutions. In what is often, revealingly, called 'the market-place of ideas', no effectual weight inheres in reasoning that is, or attempts to be, stripped of institutional interest, and that is directed towards truth for its own sake.[32]

Our times call on us to consider how we might create the conditions in which we can reason publicly in both the Kantian sense and in the general meaning of the word – that is, how we might reason as disinterested individuals and in ways that communicate successfully with others. Later I will argue that we need to create institutions that do not grant disproportionate prominence to those occupying particular institutional roles. Participatory institutions do not enforce disinterest, but they give due weight to the general interest in unencumbered truth. The implications, for both pluralism and neoliberalism, will become more obvious in the sections that follow.

Jean Jacques Rousseau noted that human nature was irreducibly dualist. The desire for personal advantage was innate in man, but so too was what he called 'the first sentiment of justice'.[33] Rousseau does not call for selflessness or self-sacrifice, but rather for an open-eyed recognition of our inescapable ambiguity as beings both narrowly self-interested and generously committed to the cause of justice. This division maps closely onto Kant's later distinction between private and public reason. The cause of general Enlightenment demands that we recognize the demands of justice even when they are inconvenient to us as institutional beings. All private forms of understanding, no matter how grand the institutions from which they derive and which they serve, must give way to the discoveries of a freely reasoning public if we are to inhabit a world safe for truth.

Kant, in distinguishing between the private and public use of reason made it clear that every public actor was also a private one, and that claims made in a private capacity must be subject to public scrutiny. And if a congregation is a private gathering, then it follows, though Kant does not say it out loud, that so is the machinery of state, in so far as its discussions are constrained by the need for obedience. Even the King is a private man when he acts in accordance with the demands of his institutional role. Kant offers the exercise of universal reason as the model of properly adult action. In place of the civic space of traditional republicanism, he insists that if we want to reason publicly we must reason without regard for the duties we normally owe to our sovereign, to our community and to ourselves as individuals with private concerns. The profoundly radical implications of Kant's approach to the question of Enlightenment perhaps explain why he was later banned from political writing. They certainly make it difficult to take seriously those British writers in particular who like to claim, as the late Professor Porter did, that 'Professor Kant's ideal of freedom was as timid as the man himself.'[34]

CHAPTER THREE

Public Servants

IN THE 1790s the established system of government in Britain came under sustained pressure. The revolutions in America and France had undermined many of the assumptions supporting monarchy and aristocracy. As Philip Harling points out, both the pressures of war and the re-emergence of religion as a force for reform play an important role in convincing political elites of the need to take into account the demands of an informed and sensible public. Pitt and later Prime Ministers recognized the need to make the administration of state business 'more accountable to an emerging public ideology shaped in part by Evangelical morality'.[1]

After the American War of Independence and in the midst of a debt crisis, the British government set up a commission to consider reforms to the system of financial administration. The commissioners invoked what they called the 'principle of public economy' and recommended a number of changes to the way civil servants were paid and government offices were organized. The commissioners argued that 'all positions in Government, including Parliament and the bureaucracy, were public trusts to be discharged for the benefit of the public, not to satisfy rights inherited or acquired by their incumbents'.[2] This reform of public appointments – the decision to see them as public, rather than as private, possessions – marks an important expansion of impersonal government.

Yet while the truth discovered by a public of private individuals occasionally lent weight to calls for legislative change, as in the campaign to abolish the slave trade, for the most part the aristocracy remained free to shape the content of state policy. Even after the expansion of the electorate in 1832, Palmerston, Gladstone and Disraeli in their different ways found the public opinion that they needed in the country through skilful electioneering, but they did so within the confines of an elite consensus. Certainly the state changed in the face of pressure from an engaged public but the partial reform of government fortified the elites by allowing them to re-imagine themselves as indispensable servants of the people. The move away from aristocratic justifications and towards arguments based on efficiency and expert knowledge in some senses provided a rationale for continued aristocratic control. Certainly it provided a powerful resource for those who resisted democratic control. As legitimacy ceases to be conferred by the Crown or secured by the excellence of an aristocratic character it comes instead to depend on particular properties of mind.

And so in an expanded franchise the aristocratic cliques that controlled the eighteenth-century Parliament, the Whigs and the Tories, reinvented themselves with little difficulty as national parties, rechristened Liberals and Conservatives. They became fluent in the language of public service and public trust and less likely openly to insist on aristocratic privilege to justify their position. Nevertheless the initiative remained with mostly aristocratic operators who reserved the right to determine the public interest. The voters ratified and legitimated decisions taken elsewhere. Politicians sought their support and approval for their platforms but the voters' role was to choose between those platforms, not to develop and promote their own. I am not sure that one voter in a hundred in the expanded electorate of the 1830s registered the significance of the opium trade both to state revenues and to the country's balance of trade. It can, however, hardly have escaped the attention of the elite, with its close ties to the East India Company and the trading interests of the City.

While those controlling the state emphasized its public character, the doctrine of *laissez-faire* in early Victorian Britain left the economy in private hands. Property owners insisted on their right to negotiate with their workforce as one individual to another and saw government regulation as an unacceptable interference in the sacred rights of contract. But by the mid-nineteenth century industrialization had expanded this private economy and the working population in the towns and cities of the industrial north and the midlands exploded. London itself grew in size from perhaps around one million in 1800 to more than six million a century later. As Hannah Arendt points out, the production of goods, which had been largely confined to the household, now took place on a massively larger scale in the quasi-public context of the factory and the mine.[3]

The complexities of urban and industrial civilization, the expansion of private industry beyond the private household, not to mention the moral enormities of unrestrained capitalism, forced the state to interfere in what had previously been considered private matters. As early as the 1830s the government had prohibited the use of children under the age of eight in the textile industry. The state did not only restrain private industry. The incapacitation of Parliament by the 'Great Stink' of 1858, not to mention a series of cholera epidemics, vividly demonstrated the limits of private planning. After all, epidemics that began in the slums, as Geoffrey Barraclough notes, had a habit of 'spreading and slaughtering tens of thousands without respect for ranks or person'.[4] The notion of 'public health' emerged as a matter of political concern in the mid-nineteenth century as the state used tax revenues on an unprecedented scale to improve the water supply.

In the second half of the nineteenth century another round of reform took place. Entrance to the civil service became conditional on success in a competitive examination in 1870 and the buying and selling of commissions in the army was abolished in 1871. Indeed, in the 1870s the relationship between the public and the private changed decisively. For the first time the 1871 trade union act legalized trade unions and a few years later picketing became legal and workers' organizations were given a public status for the first time. Rather than being treated as illegal conspirators, trade unionists were now recognized as the legitimate representatives of legitimate interests. There was also a wider pattern of interference in the private economy in the form of increased regulation and a greater willingness to use tax revenue to promote social goods, especially education.

In part, perhaps, the state moved into areas seen previously as matters for private philanthropy and the market in order to satisfy the promptings of humanitarian concern – what William Gladstone in 1887 called 'a gentler time' in which the 'public conscience' had 'grown more tender'.[5] In part it did so because industrialized and urbanized society was too complex to function without an interventionist state. But the state also abandoned *laissez-faire* and the division between the public and the private it implied in order to address the twin challenges of domestic unrest and the German Empire. Education provides a prime example. The reformer Sir James Kay Shuttleworth justified the establishment of state-funded school on the grounds that 'property would be more secure, indigence more rare, and the whole people more provident and contented if they were better educated'.[6] When Gladstone drew up plans for a national system of education it was to the Prussian model that he turned. Indeed Britain's politics of administrative and social reform after 1870 turned on the recognition that a united Germany had emerged as a serious rival to the Empire abroad and that organized labour posed a threat to the structure of society at home.

Where the claims of private property had once dovetailed neatly with the needs of state power the state now moved to intervene in the economy and in society on a much larger scale. It placed increasing emphasis on accountability, selection on merit and incorrupt administration and it justified its growing activism by insisting on its disinterested commitment to the common good. In the famous Northcote-Trevelyan report on civil service reform the authors claimed that:

> The great and increasing burden of public business . . . could not
> be carried on without an efficient body of permanent officers,
> occupying a post duly subordinate to that of Ministers . . . yet
> possessing sufficient independence, character, ability and experi-
> ence to be able to advise, assist and, to some extent, to influence
> those who are from time to time set above them.[7]

The decision to move gradually towards universal male suffrage
should be seen in the light of this increased state activism. As Benjamin
Ginsberg notes, 'electoral mobilization was closely linked to changes
in the capacity of governments to extract revenues from their
subjects'.[8] An expanding state needed more money from more of its
citizens. Giving them the vote made the state seem more a vehicle
for serving the public interest, less an instrument for entrenching the
interests of a narrow elite.

The notion of the public interest develops in Britain in ways that
move away from classical liberal ideas; the operations of the private
economy can no longer be left to deliver public goods. Instead the
state must intervene in order to maintain the country's stability and
its global pre-eminence. It does so in the name of principles of both
social justice and strategic necessity. This is not to claim that those
who pursued reform all did so as conscious agents of imperial greatness, although both Joseph Chamberlain and Charles Dilke show how
hostility to *laissez-faire* could exist alongside a close identification with
Britain's global Empire. But it became necessary to accommodate
long-standing demands for reform against a background of steadily
rising international tension. Where Locke had previously sidestepped
the state in his justification of conquest in America and relied instead
on the improving powers of private property, those who controlled
the state asserted their right to intervene in the economy to maintain
their position in the global system.

The decision to interfere in the relationship between capital and labour, to increase the state's role in education, and to expand the franchise all derive from attempts by the elite to reshape British society in the face of external competition and the threat of internal disorder. The revival of Platonism as a governing ethos in Oxford and Cambridge ties the intellectual elite to a more highly profession-alized state administration; the notion of public service expounded in the newly founded Victorian public schools binds the expanding middle class to the imperial project; the legal status granted trade unions undermines working-class radicalism by recasting the state as an institution capable of balancing competing interests. The success of public service as a device for promoting national unity can be seen in the enthusiastic response of much of the population, including much of the urban working class, to the outbreak of both the Boer War and the First World War.

The scope of state activity continues to expand into the twentieth century. After the Second World War the British state establishes a national system of healthcare and nationalizes a number of indus-tries. In the long post-war boom it appeared that the relationship between state power, capital and labour had been settled perma-nently. The idea of the 'public domain', which extended beyond the state to include the organizations of civil society, contributed to the sense that a rational and stable balance of interests had been achieved. This ideal of disinterested service to the greater good achieved a kind of apotheosis in the 1940s when the widespread acceptance of Keynesian economics combined with Keynes's own 'most character-istic belief: that public affairs should and could be managed by an elite of clever and disinterested public servants'.[9] By the 1950s the Labour politician and intellectual Anthony Crosland was still convinced that capitalism had been transformed by the public service values of the managers of large companies.[10]

Keynes, and the administrative elite of which he was part, owed a good deal to the Platonism of the late nineteenth century. The self-interested owners and the narrow-minded workers could not be expected to take the broader and more generous view of the common good. A caste of guardians was indispensable if the precarious achievements of civilization were to be preserved. According to Edward Bridges this caste needed 'much the same qualities as are called for in the academic world, namely the capacity and determination to study difficult subjects intensively and objectively, with the same disinterested desire to find the truth at all costs'.[11] In Bridges' account the modern state comes to resemble a space safe for public reasoning in Kant's sense of the word.

The ethos of public service has inspired a good deal of nostalgia in recent years and has re-emerged as a model for liberal critics of neoliberalism. For example, at the 2009 Reith Lectures the British politician Shirley Williams argued that the British and the Prussians had underpinned their societies by producing 'the modern concept of public service'. She went on to ask Michael Sandel if he thought that there was 'any chance of creating what one might call the underpinning of democratic societies without having the sense of public service revived'.[12] In the United States too, the notion that disinterested public servants should have a greater role in determining state policy has revived somewhat. Paul Krugman and Joseph Stiglitz have both called for increased regulation of the economy in the public interest. Public-spirited administrators, long seen by neoliberals as the harbingers of totalitarianism, are back in fashion.

One should, however, be wary. The idea of public service excluded most of the population from an effectively public status just as effectively as had property qualifications and the mystifications of good breeding. The concerns of citizens might be legitimate, but they themselves lacked the moral imagination and intellectual discrimination needed to strike a balance between competing claims and incommensurable goods. As the franchise expanded and the prospect of universal suffrage loomed, liberals had begun to worry about the levelling effects of majority rule. Fears about the tyrannical impulses of the majority combined with the notion of public service to justify

continued control by a social and intellectual elite. Only this classically educated caste could be trusted to reason disinterestedly and
so discover the public interest by balancing different group interests.
The individual outside the elite was assumed to be self-interested and
narrow minded. He, and later she, registered as constitutive units of
an idealized social force or as voices in the choir of a similarly idealized 'public opinion'. Public service as a doctrine very successfully
frustrated the emergence of a meaningfully sovereign public.

Broadcasting provides a good example of how a public service ethos
can shape and limit the ways in which the general population engages
with the political process. Much is sometimes made of the advantages of public service broadcasting over market-driven models. And
certainly it seems preferable to treat information as a public good to
which all citizens have broadly equal access, rather than as a private
commodity where the ability to pay secures cumulative advantages
for the wealthy. But treating information as a public good does not
ensure that individuals will receive the information and analysis that
they need for active citizenship and self-government.

From the 1920s onwards in Britain the public servants at the BBC
sought earnestly to inform and to entertain a national audience. An
assumption of cultural, intellectual and social superiority gave the
managers of this system the confidence necessary to determine what
counted as knowledge deserving of publicity. It further emboldened
them to decide on the structure of legitimate controversy without
serious or sustained attention to the views of the general population
or even the facts of the matter. In political debates, public service
broadcasters saw their role as that of representing views found in
Parliament. In the words of Stuart Hood, impartiality was understood as 'the acceptance of that segment of opinion which constitutes
parliamentary consensus'.[13] In such circumstances balance and
impartiality reliably favoured those who had secured some degree
of power already. In a society where wealth and power are distributed very unevenly the doctrine of balance will tend to favour those

already favoured while making this bias seem both natural and just. Necessarily, too, balance will marginalize information that would strengthen calls for changes to the structure of power. So, for example, Sweden's social democratic response to the economic crisis of the 1930s might as well have happened on the moon, as far as the BBC's editors at the time were concerned.

Though shaken by the spread of market forces through the broadcasting system, the BBC's managers remain convinced that they can discern what the population needs to know and that they can frame political and economic controversies in a balanced and fair way. The notion of public service helps them to see themselves as high-minded professionals. Their right to decide what receives publicity derives from their technical accomplishments, their experience and their commitment to a quite specific ideology. And so the doctrine of public service pre-empts and forestalls democratic participation in setting the agenda and broadcasting the content of journalistic inquiry. Quite understandable concerns about the impact of market forces should not blind us to the deficiencies of public service broadcasting as currently constituted.

To the extent that the public service elites of the mid-twentieth century took the concerns of the working majority into account, they did so in response to intense political pressure from popular movements outside the existing state system and the regime of private property with which it fused. The public servants delivered the welfare state only after a half-century of world war, depression and revolution. Rational administration and the balance of competing interests were tried only once every other option had been exhausted. And for all its 'independence, character, ability and experience', Bridges' administrative elite proved helpless to resist the takeover of state and society by neoliberals backed by resurgent business interests. The Thatcher administration had it in mind to 'deprivilege the Civil Service'.[14] Those who sought to remain true to their principles and to provide disinterested advice to ministers soon learned that the game had changed, and what Lord Bancroft called 'the grovel count' rose accordingly.[15] Indeed many public servants found it all too easy to reconcile their principles with the demands of the business class for deregulation and privatization. In Colin Leys's words, by the 1990s 'the higher civil service had been successfully infused with market values through changes in organization, accounting practices and promotions'.[16]

At the height of the public service ethos from the 1940s through to the 1960s, those who controlled the state remained keenly concerned to maintain their own power relative to both internal and external challengers. The demands of war and military preparedness justified the maintenance and expansion of state secrecy, and this inner core of state functions operated without the knowledge or consent of most of the population. Similarly, even after nationalization, the Bank of England remains central to a system of finance that escapes popular comprehension and is therefore well placed to shake off efforts to restrain it. Those who sincerely believed that they were serving the public interest also believed that the masses had only a very limited mandate to give them instructions. For the most part, the public service ethos co-existed with a very narrow understanding of democracy as an 'institutional arrangement for arriving at political decisions in which individuals acquire the power to decide by means of a competitive struggle for the people's vote'.[17] Those who organized the knowledge on which political decisions were based had no more interest in an active public than did the industrial and commercial interests that continued to exert a vastly disproportionate influence over the content of policy. The ethos of public service shaded into an ethos of service to a state whose inner workings and motivations remained deeply mysterious. Edward Bridges, one of the most important exemplars of the public service tradition, exemplified the blurring of the two when in the course of one lecture he remarked that civil service work contributed to 'the continued well-being of the state' and, in a separate passage, to 'the continued well-being of the community'.[18]

There was, then, a paradoxical quality to the state in the decades before the neoliberal turn. Its objectives remained largely beyond general comprehension, even as those who controlled it prided themselves on their service to the public. The public sector expanded, as did the share of national income spent by the state. But the population at large had little knowledge of, or control over, the institutions that operated in their name. They had correspondingly little interest in defending the very real technical achievements of Keynes' civilized men and women. There is no reason to think that a revival of the notion of the public service, however desirable, will suffice as a response to the current shambles.

CHAPTER FOUR

The American Republic

THE POLITICAL CULTURE of Britain's American colonies – and, later, of the United States – diverged sharply from that of Britain itself. Many settlers had brought with them republican and Puritan ideas of self-government in godly communities. Furthermore, the vast scale of the territory open to English settlement and the relative weakness of foreign competitors, especially after the defeat of the French by the British in the mid-eighteenth century, meant that there was little need for a strong state of the sort that had developed in the old country. Attempts by Britain to introduce landlords, tenant farmers and landless labourers failed in the face of squatting on a grand scale. Indeed Britain's failure to introduce an idealized form of the landlordism that prevailed at home established the conditions for both general enrichment and independent economic development. Long after the middling farmers who had secured victory for Parliament in the Civil War had vanished, and long after enclosure in England had removed the common resources that underpinned traditions of popular and collective management, the American Republic continued to think of itself in terms derived from the rhetoric of the English Civil War. It was fortunate for America that Locke's 1669 constitution for Carolina, with its aristocratic grades and insistence on social stability – 'All the children of Leet-men shall be Leet-men, and so to all Generations'[1] – proved equal parts wishful thinking and gobbledygook.

The so-called 'permanent settlement' in India established a British system of land tenure far more successfully, with dreadful consequences for the majority of the rural population. The British mixed a ruthless insistence on the rights of private landlords, a super-charged version of *laissez-faire* and a whimsically romantic attitude towards social forms in India that they systematically misunderstood. The pernicious effects of cultural differences and geographical distance permitted the British administration to allow market forces to cause even more damage than in the home country. Over a period of more than 150 years the country suffered repeated famines while the British state derived stupendous material benefits and its public servants marvelled at their own humane disinterest. That this process of extractive administration was presided over by a tiny number of classicists who gloried in the name of 'guardians' provides yet another reason to be wary of bureaucratic Platonism.

In its early decades the federal government that replaced the Crown in the United States made few inroads into traditions of local and regional self-government. Thomas Jefferson could sound very much like Harrington when he invoked the republican virtues of the independent farmer. Indeed he could even echo Winstanley when he declared that 'the earth is given as a common stock for man to labor and live on'.[2] The power exerted by the various Jeffersonian publics was essentially negative. They were able to prevent the permanent establishment of a central bank and a standing army and thus denied the federal government the means to engage in great-power politics.

This is not to gloss over the Republic's flaws. The effective restriction of the centre permitted any number of abuses to survive in the states. The weakness of the central government allowed slavery to flourish, long after it had become an outrage to majority opinion in the country as a whole. Many frontier communities combined a refreshing contempt for efforts to reduce them to landless labourers with a vicious hostility to the native inhabitants of the areas they settled. Despite the terrible crimes committed against the native peoples and the obscenity of slavery, the many regional publics were able to prevent the central state from conducting itself in a manner that ran contrary to their wishes. They remained immune to the language of national greatness and satisfied themselves with their own affairs. In many cases republican government achieved a scale and sophistication never seen before on earth, to the extent that the American of the early Republic seemed to European observers to represent a new kind of man. Their lived experience of civic freedom prompted Lord Byron to remark that he would rather 'have a nod from an American than a snuffbox from an emperor'.[3] The reality of the early years of the United States was sufficiently glorious, and marked a sufficiently golden contrast with the experience of the British in particular during the same period, that it inspired a powerful strain of political idealism both at the time and in later generations.

But republican rule, in which men deliberated as formal equals on matters of common concern, depended on reliable access to the information necessary for self-government, as well as knowledge of the men they elected as their representatives, and a high degree of economic autonomy. As such it sat uneasily with the facts of continental expansion and economic consolidation. The emergence of great industrial combines and the centralizing impact of a series of wars tested, apparently to destruction, the republican assumptions that had informed American political culture. In the early twentieth century the economist Simon Patten noted with something approaching relief that 'during the last sixty years the individual has been lost'.[4] Small-scale enterprises with little power to determine prices or to lobby government ceded more and more ground to large corporations that came to make a farce of liberal assumptions about the workings of markets and the divisions between the economic and the political sphere. Rewards for talent and application began to pale when compared with those that flowed to shrewd corruption and the manipulation of opinion.

Just before the outbreak of the First World War, in the ominously entitled *The New Freedom*, Woodrow Wilson highlighted the shift away from the politics of personal familiarity: 'Today the everyday relationships of men are largely with great impersonal concerns, not with other individual men. Now this is nothing short of a new social age, a new era of human relationships, a new stage-setting for the human drama.'[5] And for the most part men dealt with one kind of impersonal concern and did so in a very specific way: 'There was a time when corporations played a very minor part in our business affairs, but now they play the chief part, and most men are the servants of corporations.'[6] Economic life ceased to be a lesson in the rigours of individual autonomy and a preparation for a clear-sighted, if self-interested, politics. By the 1930s it seemed that 'the extreme division of labour in large scale enterprise' implied 'not individualism but cooperation and the acceptance of authority almost to the point of autocracy'.[7]

Wilson didn't want to resist or roll back the 'Great Society' created by industrialization and urban expansion. Corporations were reckoned necessary to modern industrial organization and their rights to citizenship increasingly came to seem natural and unobjectionable. As far as Wilson and the mainstream progressives were concerned, to challenge the dominant trends in American society was to succumb to anarchism or socialism. The issue was not whether it was possible to transform this 'Great Society' into something consistent with republican democracy. The issue was how republican democracy could be transformed into something that did not obstruct these new and self-evidently progressive developments. The solution lay in an improved and strengthened central administration.

Walter Lippmann enjoyed a stellar career as the anatomist of the problems created by the new and vast scale of the American system. In his 1922 book *Public Opinion*, he presented an influential critique of the conventional wisdom concerning popular sovereignty and proposed a programme of institutional reform that would bring his country much closer to the British approach to state power.

His argument begins by rejecting the dogmatic belief of the democratic idealist that 'somehow mysteriously there exists in the hearts of men a knowledge of the world beyond their reach'.[8] He argued that 'spontaneous democracy', where casual experience supplies the information the citizen needs to exercise sovereignty, depends on conditions that 'approximate those of the isolated rural township'.[9]

Far from accessing reality through some mysterious instinct, citizens in an industrial society relied on what Lippmann called a 'pseudo-environment' created by the media for information about the wider world. Citizens were still nominally the governors of this wider world. But the media businesses on which they relied were poorly equipped for the work of informing public opinion. Newspapers were businesses that must hang on to readers, by any and all means necessary. Objective reporting of 'the dull important' had to take its chances alongside 'the curious trivial . . . the hunger for sideshows and three-legged calves'.[10] Audiences that weren't sidetracked by three-legged calves still struggled to see the world clearly: 'for the most part we do not first see, and then define, we define first and then see'.[11] What Lippmann calls stereotypical thinking helps us make sense of 'the great blooming, buzzing confusion of reality'. More than that, 'it is the guarantee of our self-respect'.[12] Stereotypes, patterns of association and prejudice, 'unconscious constellations of feeling',[13] enable us to make sense of the world at the cost of misunderstanding it. For most of us, most of the time, Lippmann argues, it is a cost we are willing to bear.

The solution was to dispense with unrealistic optimism about what the public was capable of. We shouldn't pretend that citizens are omnicompetent. Rather we should give citizens a political role better suited to their abilities and limitations. The population is competent to assess the record of their representatives in delivering specified goods, on the basis of plainly recorded and objectively measured criteria. The legitimate test of insiders by outsiders is whether they have done a good job delivering 'a certain minimum of health, of decent housing, of material necessities, of education, of freedom, of pleasures, of beauty'. Government was a matter of managerial competence, not of vibrating to 'the self-centred opinions that happen to be floating about in men's minds'. Yet in the absence of institutions that relay 'the realities of public life . . . the common interests very largely elude public opinion entirely'.[14]

If the population do not themselves have the knowledge needed to formulate policy, and can only pass judgement on a government's performance in retrospect, who then will provide government with the information it needs? Lippmann's answer in large part accounts for his book's success. A new group of disinterested experts would supply 'governments, schools, newspapers and churches' with 'a reliable picture of the world'.[15] This reliable picture of the world would then be transmitted down to the population: 'public opinions must be organized for the press if they are to be sound, not by the press as is the case today'.[16]

In other words, 'public opinion' remains, but its meaning changes radically. The knowledge that informs policy doesn't spring from the hearts of a spontaneously informed citizenry, nor can it be entrusted to the press. Public opinion must be formulated by 'men who are not personally involved, who control enough facts, and have the dialectical skill to sort out what is real perception from what is stereotype, pattern and elaboration'. Lippmann promises his readers that a governmental system of organized inquiry 'would become the focus of information of the most extraordinary kind'.[17] A caste of Platonic guardians will boil away the fat of stereotypical thinking and provide the governing institutions with the knowledge that they need. In exchange they will eat the fruit of the tree of this national organization of knowledge and come to know the subtle pleasures of inside information.

As the responsibilities of America expanded to encompass the globe, the population would no longer generate public opinion spontaneously. It would receive it from these new producers of disinterested knowledge. Voters could then, on the basis of the opinions provided for them, decide whether to keep the representatives they had, or to choose some others: 'The public must be put in its place, so that it may exercise its own powers, but no less and perhaps even more so, so that each of us may live free of the trampling and the roar of a bewildered herd.' When Lippmann talks of his new directorate of disinterested experts he has in mind something akin to the British foreign office – 'the best diplomatic service in the world', since it makes 'the most complete separation between the assembly of knowledge and the control of policy'.[18] And his admiration for the British system of administration points to his wider ambitions. Lippmann, I think, wanted America to leave behind its sullen and insular adolescence as a Republic and take up its adult calling as a great empire.

Public Opinion and its sequel, *The Phantom Public*, exerted a considerable influence on the development of the United States. Lippmann's success can be explained in part by his covert appeal to the interests of those who would become the privileged administrators of this new national system of knowledge. But he also benefited from a central, organizing ambiguity in his treatment of ends and means. Throughout his work Lippmann plausibly insists that no individual can possibly acquire the vast store of knowledge needed to comprehend the details of public policy. In *The Phantom Public* he asks satirically how the concerned citizen should divide his time between matters as diverse as the Brooklyn subways, the Manchurian railways, Britain's rights in the Sudan and rural credits in Montana.[19]

But while a division of labour in complex political systems is a necessity, the critical question is where this division is to be made. Lippmann believed that a single apparatus of decision could decide both the ends and the means of political action. The state, assisted by science, could supply its own goals and determine how to achieve them. Expert insiders could be trusted to provide an accurate picture of the world to both political decision-makers and public opinion.

The public would then judge the performance of elected officials on the basis of this same information.

However, while the details of administration might escape any individual, the aims of the state cannot safely be left to any group of insiders. No neutral process of observation and analysis can determine the objectives of policy. The aims of the state are matters of desire, they are not facts about the world. And to believe that the ordinary, and ordinarily distracted, citizen can conceive of the world she wishes for herself and for her children is not to succumb to any democratic dogma that I can see. For all its tone of worldly realism, Lippmann's anti-democratic rhetoric rests at last on nothing more substantial than a great buzzing confusion of terms. His confidence that a state apparatus insulated from the general population and empowered to supply the content of public opinion can be trusted amounts to a kind of power worship.

Lippmann's proposal to clarify public opinion by a national organization of knowledge chimed not only with the interests of would-be philosopher-administrators. It also suited the few thousand owners and managers who controlled the new corporations and the rapidly expanding financial sector. The corporations and the banks provided the state with much of its personnel while the grant-giving foundations set up by the Rockefeller family and its imitators shaped the organizing assumptions of the social sciences in the United States. The responsibility for forming public opinion would be given to men who doubtless considered themselves neutral and rational, but whose elevation had depended on their exquisite sensitivity to very particular interests.

At the same time as Lippmann was writing *Public Opinion*, Edward Bernays was offering an unillusioned account, leavened by salesmanship, of how the organization of public opinion would be conducted. In a series of articles and books Bernays also insisted that most people were incapable of political autonomy of the sort assumed by democratic theory. Rather like Locke, Bernays believed that those who could not think should be made to believe by a dedicated cadre of experts. Using the dynamics of human psychology, these experts would act as engineers of public opinion, directing the desires that 'are the steam that makes the social machine work'.[20] In Bernays's view, only a tiny minority of enlightened individuals could discern the needs of society as a whole, and so should develop new techniques of manipulation to secure the consent or compliance of the majority. With unusual candour he outlined how this minority could control a formally democratic society through the active management of public opinion. And he insisted on the need to do so: 'ours must be a leadership democracy administered by the intelligent minority who know how to regiment and guide the masses'.[21]

The public relations ideology that Bernays helped to create takes the population to be an unstable mass that must be directed or dosed into the correct states of mind by clinically minded professionals. Its very name is a lie, in so far as the industry does not seek to engage with a public but rather to prevent any public from emerging, or else to reduce any that do exist to objects of manipulation for their clients through the imaginative expenditure of money.

Bernays did everything he could to enhance his reputation as an all-powerful manipulator. His claims to be able to manage the masses scientifically were in part a sales pitch. But Bernays played an important role in developing the public relations industry's governing principles and techniques. For example, he outlined the distinction between 'continuous interpretation' and 'dramatization by high-spotting' – that is, between the steady management of the mass mind and the creation of dramatic, reinforcing events. He insisted on the need for the propagandist to study 'systematically and objectively the material with which he is working in the spirit of the laboratory'.[22] And he brilliantly outlined existing social hierarchies and patterns of subordination that a gifted propagandist could turn to his advantage.[23] Bernays largely deserves his reputation as the founding father of propaganda understood as 'the executive arm of the invisible government'.[24]

Graham Wallas had pointed out just before the First World War that if the wealthy were to set aside a third of their income to promote and defend their interests 'there is so much skill to be bought, and the art of using skill for the production of emotion and opinion is so advanced that the whole condition of electoral contests would be changed for the future'.[25] Bernays and his peers were able to reassure the rich that effective control of popular opinion could extend far beyond the electoral process and could be had for far less money than Wallas had imagined.

The educator and political theorist John Dewey responded to the problems Lippmann explored with an account of the public and its relationship with the state that drew heavily on the republican experience of America in the eighteenth and nineteenth centuries. Dewey accepted the outlines of Lippmann's diagnosis; writing in 1927 he too worried that methods of self-government emerging from direct communication between members of a defined community had been outpaced by rapid changes in industrial technology and organization. But he rejected the cure proposed.

While Dewey recognized that the scale of industrial America rendered self-governing communities increasingly peripheral, he worried that in the new impersonal conditions deceptive and manipulative groups could secure effective control of the state for their own ends. He therefore proposed that the 'Great Society' of impersonal organization be balanced by what he called a 'great community'. This 'great community' would be possible only if local communities and the habits of face-to-face exchange found there could be revived – 'the local community is the medium in which a vast but dormant intelligence can be made articulate and intelligible'.[26]

As things stood, 'the new era of human relationships' had 'no political agencies worthy of it' and 'the democratic public' remained 'largely inchoate and unorganized'.[27] Major changes would be necessary if the newly industrial society was to have institutions capable of controlling it in the public interest. Though the talk of a 'great community' can make Dewey sound a little unworldly, there was a hard edge to his response his era's crisis of publicity, as when he acknowledged that 'to form itself the public has to break existing political forms'.[28]

Dewey's crisis is in large part ours. His insistence on the central importance of human association to the creation of effective publics remains important and true, and we will return to it later in the book. It may not be clear precisely what Dewey had in mind when he talked of a 'great community', but his instinct to seek the resources for reform in the traditions of republican self-government was, I think, sound. Still, it was Lippmann who had the greater influence on the development of the American state and indeed his *Public Opinion* stands as one of the most important events in the history of the decline of the American Republic.

The shift from a network of agrarian publics to an urban, industrial and corporate society was very sudden, and – compounded by the confusion of war and depression and the giddy achievement of a global pre-eminence – still has to be fully registered by many Americans. As a result, the town hall meeting has retained a powerful mystique and continues to provide an important method for reaching the population and persuading it that it continues to exist as a public. What might be called republican publics have endured as both a lived reality, albeit for a shrinking percentage of the population, and as an image in the culture industry broadly defined – one thinks of the carefully staged informality of the New Hampshire primaries and the television coverage they generate.[29] But the town hall meeting and the wider republican tradition have long been targets of successful manipulation from above. In the months after America declared war on Germany and Austria in 1917, the Commission on Public Information (CPI) had trained and managed some 75,000 'Four Minute Men' who delivered carefully themed addresses to the local meetings held to discuss matters of common concern.

The persistence of the republican vision of American society offered an inspiring, if finally empty, alternative to working-class radicalism. The municipal heroism celebrated by Frank Capra in *It's a Wonderful Life* and *Mr Smith Goes to Washington*, for example, left intact an idea of individual distinction that resonated strongly with the country's republican habits of sentiment. Needless to say, those who peddled this vision of small-town virtue most energetically also worked to accelerate the destruction of the independent farmers and small-business owners who had provided the backbone of the republican body politic. Most recently, Sarah Palin's rhetoric has effectively exploited a half-remembered Republic of small towns, while her support for unrestrained corporate expansion in Wasilla, and the town's well-known status as the methamphetamine capital of Alaska, suggests a somewhat different order of priorities.

The management of public opinion outlined by Lippmann and Bernays achieved a brief and unstable supremacy in the United States in the 1920s, helped by a vicious campaign of repression against Bolshevism, anarchism and radical trade unionism. Academics and financiers together hailed the arrival of a new economy of unlimited growth and venerated the market as representing 'everything everybody knows, hopes, believes, anticipates'.[30] Critics retreated into a sophisticated ennui, what Edmund Wilson later called 'the mad hilarity and tragedy of jazz'.[31] The Wall Street Crash and the ensuing worldwide depression did not put an end to the idea that insiders should shape public opinion, but the Roosevelt administration, animated by fear of both revolution and counter-revolution, worked with the leaders of popular organizations, including the labour movement, and granted the unions a public status through New Deal legislation, particularly the Wagner Act of 1935. Central to the New Deal response to the economic crisis was the belief that 'the liberty of democracy is not safe if the people tolerate the growth of private power to a point where it becomes stronger than the democratic state'. President Roosevelt told Congress in 1938 that 'ownership of government by an individual, by a group, or by any other controlling private power' was fascist.[32] Here we see the origins of the post-war settlement as a balance of contending interests.

Both the success of the New Deal in preserving constitutional government and victory in the Second World War contributed to a sense that American society had achieved a lasting balance between the interests of workers and owners. In 1960 the sociologist Seymour Lipset wrote that:

> The fundamental problems of the industrial revolution have been solved: the workers have achieved industrial and political citizenship; the conservatives have accepted the welfare state; and the democratic left has recognized that an increase in over-all state power carries with it more dangers to freedom than solutions to economic problems.

This was the age of 'the end of ideology' and the triumph of pluralism, the belief that 'the views of citizens are effectively and equitably represented through competing organized interests'.[33] In the account of American politics offered by the pluralists, interest groups assemble and attempt to influence wider public opinion and the legislative process. These groups compete to secure action from an impartial state and form *ad hoc* coalitions of convenience in pursuit of their aims. The public interest is discovered through the conflicts between organized interests as reported in a competitive and broadly reliable media system.

In this free-for-all no particular interest group can expect to secure a dominant position over other groups in society. According to the pluralist account, 'there is no single center of sovereign power', rather there are 'multiple centers of power, none of which is or can be wholly sovereign'. And since 'one center of power is set against another, power itself will be tamed, civilized, controlled, and limited to decent human purposes'.[34] According to pluralists the political process is 'incredibly complex' and 'any simple theory about how American citizens influence the conduct of their government is bound to be misleading'.[35]

Though pluralism became the dominant political theory of the post-war era in the United States, and also exerted considerable influence in Britain, there are a number of problems with it. For a start, the emphasis on organized interest groups had the peculiar effect of removing the disinterested citizen from the field of political activity. If the views and interests of citizens could be represented adequately by organized groups, then the heads of business lobbies, professional associations and trade unions could be left to discover the public interest together. Pluralism celebrated the eclipse of the ideal of disinterested reason as a guide for political action as far as the majority of the population was concerned. Only those who held a private position as the representative of a defined group would be able effectively to discuss matters of public concern. In this respect, pluralism's assumptions dovetailed with the ideals of public service in Britain. Everyone, apart from the caste of liberal and reasonable administrators who controlled the state, was self-interested, and stability was to be achieved by balancing their competing interests.

Accordingly, pluralism assumed that the state was neutral in this struggle between organized groups. At times this assumption could turn simultaneously comic and sinister. Daniel Bell, the most prominent advocate of the idea that ideological struggle had been replaced by the management of the claims of organized interest groups, angrily rejected suggestions that in fact conjoined elites in business and the state together dominated American society. He chose to launch his assault on 'vulgar sociology' in the pages of *Encounter*, an impeccably liberal and pluralist publication covertly funded by the CIA. The idea that serious ideological disagreements had been replaced by what Bell himself called 'a rough consensus among intellectuals on political issues: the acceptance of a Welfare State; the desirability of decentralized power; a system of mixed economy and of political pluralism'[36] was itself a prominent feature of the American state's efforts to influence European and domestic opinion. In the complex world of pluralism, too great an emphasis on the coordinating power of a far-from-neutral state would lead to accusations of simple-mindedness. If, on the other hand, you were sophisticated enough to embrace pluralism, the CIA would gladly fund your magazine.

The state, not surprisingly, continued to favour those groups that strengthened it relative to other states and to internal threats. Those groups seeking to transform the state in fundamental ways were not treated even-handedly, and the absence of serious ideological controversy by the late 1950s was achieved through the energetic suppression of dissent in academia and the labour movement. Intellectuals who doubted that ideology had been replaced by minor disagreements about the balance between market forces and state planning lost their jobs. Similarly, labour leaders who survived the McCarthy reaction fought hard for their members' interests, but did so while accepting the structure of industrial organization. Business leaders respected and feared the union leader George Meany, but they appreciated that he was 'a big opponent of socialism'. Indeed, one businessman remarked with some relief that 'American labor is the most conservative in the world. They don't care about participation in management.'[37]

Pluralism also assumed that alliances in civil society were constantly shifting. But while businesses competed and different sectors had conflicting interests, those who controlled industry had overwhelmingly more coordinated power to resist threats to their common interests. For example, through their advertising budgets they ensured that the privately owned media worked hard in their long-term interests. When the president of CBS, Frank Stanton, confided that 'since we are advertiser-supported we must take into account the general objectives and desires of the advertisers as a whole', he was doing no more than stating the obvious.[38] Whatever the pluralists imagined, business was not anarchic, the state was not neutral, and the media were not impartial.

Still, the experts and administrators of the pluralist era in the United
States and Britain tended to see in the post-war settlement something approaching the best of all possible worlds, a self-evidently just
and therefore durable settlement. They were not inclined to register
the fact that the notions of public service to which they subscribed –
together with the doctrine of a balance of domestic interests and the
need for cooperation and compromise between capital and labour
above all – were not inevitable consequences of the operations of
political reason but the product of trends towards incorrupt administration and the accommodation of organized labour that were
inseparable from the realities of revolution and war. The control of
the state by largely liberal experts seemed as natural and pleasing to
the experts themselves as it seemed both reasonable and just. And in
the post-war period the architects of the New Deal state did not set
out to create a vision of a social democratic society in alliance with
the trade unions. Instead they concentrated on redistributing wealth
from an unreconstructed private sector into social programmes that
they themselves would administer. In both the United States and
Britain, liberal intellectuals and the democratic left largely accepted
the principles of Cold War confrontation and showed little interest in
broadening popular participation in decision-making.

Though the experts had secured the degree of influence they
enjoyed as a consequence of the power of organized labour, and
the threat that it posed to the state, no lasting alliance resulted.
The population was to be helped, but all too often they were seen
as a mass to be improved rather than as the originators of political change. Bernays's progeny in the public relations industry loved
pluralism since it allowed them to portray the steady triumph of their
clients' interests, and the gradual weakening of organized labour, as
the unpredictable outcomes of a chaotic melee. After all, wasn't it
simple-minded or conspiratorial to imagine otherwise? Meanwhile,
the notion that the heads of representative groups in society could
together hammer out a consensus on what constituted the public

interest gave the system a steadily manipulative character; constituencies became objects of administration while the heads of other groups came to seem like collaborators. Forgetting or not knowing why they occupied the positions they did, the advocates of the pluralist state were confused and demoralized when what they had assumed to be a lasting compromise was swept away.

It is against this background of a reluctance to distinguish between interest groups, to find patterns of collaboration between them, to look steadily at the federal state, or to provide an accurate account of the hierarchy of power in the American system, that C. Wright Mills sketched his distinction between the public and the mass. Drawing on the same models of republican life as Dewey, Mills located the distinction in four key areas. First, 'the ratio of givers of opinion to the receivers'[39] differs between the two. The archetype of public communication is a conversation between two people; the broadcast of one person's voice to an audience of millions is the archetype of mass communication. In a public, 'virtually as many people express opinions as receive them'. Second, 'public communications are so organized that there is a chance immediately and effectively to answer back any opinion expressed in public' and citizens can respond to what they are told without fear of reprisal. In the perfectly realized mass society, even private dissent carries penalties and open disagreement is forbidden. Third, a public has the means to translate its opinion into 'effective action' while a mass has no such means. Finally, in a public perfectly realized, 'no agent of formal authority moves among the autonomous public', while in a mass society 'the public is terrified into uniformity by the infiltration of informers and the universalization of suspicion'.[40]

A public can be distinguished from a mass most readily, Mills argues, by their respectively characteristic forms of communication: a public proceeds by discussion while a mass is held in position ('crystallised' is Bernays's term) by the operations of the media. Indeed, as he puts it, 'the publics become mere media markets: all those exposed to the contents of given mass media'.[41] Already by the 1950s Mills thought that any reasonable observer would have to acknowledge that his country was far removed from the model assumed by pluralism, and was well on the way to becoming a mass society.[42] Later developments have vindicated him, and left his many contemporary critics looking hopelessly complacent.[43]

CHAPTER FIVE

Neoliberal Publics

B Y THE MID-1970s the public service ethos in Britain and the pluralist conception of politics in the United States were in a state of crisis. The return of popular militancy in the 1960s shook the confidence of liberal elites in the state administration and of the business class. Meanwhile the economy was no longer delivering the growth that had bankrolled the post-war condominium of capital and labour. Keynesian technicians of the mixed economy seemed helpless in the face of these problems and increasingly lost intellectual ground to a resurgent 'new right' calling for policies that would embolden private investors and thereby restore growth.

Public servants and liberal administrators had become used to acting on behalf of the general population, rather than at its behest. Attempts to engineer society by technocratic *fiat* replaced drives for reform in the inter-war years that had developed out of popular experience and desire for change and had found expression in a powerful labour movement. The defenders of the existing settlement seemed unable to offer a general account of the public interest that resonated like right-wing rhetoric about getting government out of the way. At the same time, radical calls from the left for extensive reform of capitalism and increased democratic control over economic decision-making convinced business elites that their continued supremacy was in doubt. The following decades would mark a largely successful effort by those who owned and managed the private economy to reshape the legal environment and the constitution of ideas. The power of private property was used to discredit or marginalize the ideals of public service, as notions of a mixed economy were driven out of respectable intellectual society.

The change in attitude among senior managers in the mid-1970s is well captured in a series of interviews collected by Leonard Silk and David Vogel in 1976, published under the title *Ethics and Profits: The Crisis of Confidence in American Business*. The mood at the time of the bicentenary was grim. One businessman warned that 'if we don't take action now we will see our own demise'.[1] Another complained that 'we are like the head of a household, and the public sector is like our wife and children. They can only consume what we produce.'[2] The post-war emphasis on redistribution of wealth, as opposed to institutional change, allowed the business elite, still in place but insecure, to justify their fight back in terms of sensible household management. Private enterprise was the breadwinner, the providing father. If the head of household was to avert social breakdown, or a loss of status, which was from his perspective the same thing, the rest of the family would have to be put in its place. A largely white, male and middle-aged business elite was feeling increasingly threatened by the new assertiveness of women, minorities and the young.

In the 1940s and 1950s those who had demanded greater participation in management and democratic oversight of the economy had been attacked as stooges of Soviet Russia and marginalized in the post-war settlement. Private owners had agreed to state regulation in return for retaining control of the enterprise; in a typical formulation from the 1940s, Ken Wells, the head of the Advertising Council, had accepted 'government regulation but not government control'.[3] Now that the economy appeared to be struggling, industry spent huge sums to persuade Americans of the need to dismantle the system of controls established after the Second World War. Reagan's rhetoric – 'in this present crisis, government is not the solution' – became persuasive thanks to this lavish background orchestration.[4] The insistence of the business class on their right to govern, and their ability to communicate their favoured messages, was based on their continued control of the productive economy.

Silk and Vogel noted how 'criticism of the one man, one vote principle surfaced innumerable times' at business conferences, though 'hardly any executives or businessmen would question them publicly'.[5] Distrust of the political process went hand in hand with a delight in the democratic possibilities of the market-place. The authors quote one businessman convinced that 'in a market-place, every person gets a vote every day. The market is more democratic than the government.'[6] This long-standing staple of business propaganda – it dates back to the 1930s campaigns against planning – was to become the central tenet of the renewed faith among business leaders of their right to defeat domestic challenges to their authority. Its effectiveness as propaganda derived in part from the fact that so many businessmen believed it quite sincerely.

Concern about political activism among groups that had previously been passive, and the need to suppress the political ambitions of women, minorities and the young, provide the central themes in Samuel Huntington's contribution to *The Crisis of Democracy*, a collection of essays put together in 1975 by the Trilateral Commission. Huntington worried that the operations of democracy itself 'appear to have generated a breakdown of traditional means of social control, a delegitimation of social and other kinds of authority, and an overload of demands on government, exceeding its capacity to respond'.[7] The population now wanted more from government and this was interfering with the projects of those who had normally enjoyed unimpeded access to the state's resources. The culprits were those who had hitherto maintained a respectful distance from the business of politics – 'previously passive or unorganized groups in the population now embarked on concerted efforts to establish their claims to opportunities, positions, rewards, and privileges, which they had not considered themselves entitled to before'. The groups causing this trouble sound remarkably like those denied a public status in the seventeenth century – women, blacks, and propertyless men:

> Blacks and women made impressive gains in their representation in state legislatures and Congress . . . In a similar vein there was a marked expansion of white collar unionism and of the readiness and willingness for clerical, technical, and professional employees in public and private bureaucracies to assert themselves and to secure protection for their rights and privileges.[8]

And in this they were aided by 'intellectuals and related groups who assert their disgust with the corruption, materialism, and inefficiency of democracy and with the subservience of democratic government to "monopoly capitalism"'.[9] At one point in the text the authors warn that these new 'value-oriented intellectuals' constitute 'a challenge to democratic government which is, potentially at least, as serious as those posed in the past by the aristocratic cliques, fascist movements, and communist parties'.[10] The suggestion that left-wing academics might pose as serious a threat to democracy as Nazism must count as one of the more startling productions of America's, often baroque, culture of political paranoia.

Still, some intellectuals had been showing a troubling lack of deference. In the summer of 1962 a group called Students for a Democratic Society had published *The Port Huron Statement*. In it they called for 'the establishment of a democracy of individual participation'. This was to be governed by two central aims. First, each individual would 'share in those social decisions determining the quality and direction of his life'; second 'society [would] be organized to encourage independence in men and provide the media for their common participation'. The authors were conscious of the role that political activity played in the full expression of our human capacities: 'politics has the function of bringing people out of isolation into community, thus being a necessary, though not sufficient, means of finding meaning in social life'. Furthermore it was a 'root principle' of participatory democracy that 'decision-making of basic human consequence be carried on by public groupings'.[11] Perhaps most ominously, *The Port Huron Statement* asked how the public sector might be truly public 'and not the arena of a ruling bureaucracy of "public servants"'.[12] The public servants at the FBI began infiltrating student organizations the following year and launched a full-blown counter-intelligence programme against the New Left in October of 1968.[13]

Popular attitudes towards business and government had become markedly more sceptical in the years before the publication of *The Crisis of Democracy*. In 1971 a poll by *PR Reporter* had found that 61 per cent of respondents agreed that 'too few companies had too much power'. Almost half of those asked (45 per cent) thought that 'large companies should be broken up'.[14] In the previous year the University of Michigan's Survey Research Centre found that 'trust in government' had fallen to very low levels. Howard Zinn notes that there 'was a significant difference by class. Of professional people, 40 per cent had "low" political trust in the government; of unskilled blue-collar workers, 66 per cent had "low" trust'.[15] Industry would spend a billion dollars a year between 1975 and 1980 to reshape distrust of government and big business into a celebration of individual freedom and a campaign against regulation.[16] Popular hostility towards the military-industrial state would be repackaged into resentment of meddling liberals and of what the public relations expert Philip Lesly called 'that traditional source of scapegoats, the isolated and oppressed'.[17]

Huntington thought that the new found confidence of previously excluded groups amounted to an 'excess of democracy' or a 'democratic distemper'.[18] In this his language notably echoed that of the seventeenth-century English republican Thomas Gordon, who warned that free states could all too easily be overcome by 'a Distemper arising from too much health'.[19] Huntington had two suggestions as to how this distemper might be treated:

First, democracy is only one way of constituting authority, and it is not necessarily a universally applicable one. In many situations the claims of expertise, experience, and special talents may override the claims of democracy as a way of constituting authority. Second, *the effective operation of a democratic political system usually requires some measure of apathy and non-involvement on the part of some individuals and groups.*[20]

The coalition that had run the United States would reassert itself by creating new forms of 'expertise', by rediscovering old ones, and by celebrating the 'special talents' of those who were fit to rule. Groups that challenged their control of the state were driven back into apathy and isolation as the business community exploited its control of the productive economy to subsidize a radical shift in the economy of ideas, attacking the notion of public service and exalting the dynamism of what they insisted on calling free markets. The image of an overbearing and sclerotic state was to be contrasted with supposedly fluid and democratic markets, even as in reality the state became ever more efficient in delivering profits to the corporate sector and passing costs onto the wider population.

The capture of the executive in both Britain and the United States in 1979–1980 led in the years that followed to a radical shift in the very idea of the public interest. Politicians and civil servants no longer needed to intervene in markets in the wider interests of the community. Market forces left to themselves would deliver the public interest. In fact, markets were the only safe way to discover the public interest. In the decades that followed, the idea of the public interest as something distinct from the outcome of market forces progressively vanished from both the general culture and the terms of legislation.[21] According to the new conventional wisdom the very idea of a public domain was a myth. In an interview with *Woman's Own* magazine, Margaret Thatcher famously insisted that 'there is no such thing as society. There are individual men and women, and there are families.'[22] Appeals to the common good were fraudulent unless they were also calls for greater freedom for individuals in unregulated markets.

As Huntington hoped, new forms of expertise emerged to reinforce these claims. In the United States, James Buchanan's 'public choice theory' influentially applied the assumptions of classical economics to the political sphere. In the world of public choice theory, politicians, administrators and voters are straightforwardly self-seeking. As in neoclassical economic theory, man is taken to be 'an egoistic, rational, utility maximizer'.[23] Whatever they may claim, politicians are driven by the desire to secure and keep the satisfactions of office; bureaucrats want bigger budgets, more responsibility and an ever wider scope to impose their will. Voters choose the candidates that promise to give them the material goods they want. Buchanan's work sought to characterize the idea that individuals could identify and serve the public interest as a kind of political romanticism. The public interest was simply what served the interests of public servants.

In the light of public choice theory, voting famously became irrational. Since everyone's vote was no more than an expression of individual self-interest, and no individual could possibly expect their vote to be decisive in an electoral contest involving many thousands or millions of voters, there was no point in voting. As if in admiring imitation of business propaganda that recast consumption as direct democracy, public choice theory transformed voting into a defective prototype for shopping.

In Britain the alleged insights of the neoliberal right provided useful background justifications for a radical restructuring of the state. Since government officials were self-seeking and apt to stifle private competition to secure rents for themselves, the deregulation of private industry and the privatization of state-owned enterprises powerfully recommended themselves. Public choice theory inspired the so-called 'New Public Management' and its assault on the ideals of public service.

In the mid-1970s the state sector had produced around a fifth of the national wealth.[24] By the mid-1990s almost all of the state's productive capacity had been sold off. In an exhaustive study of privatization in Britain, *The Great Divestiture*, Massimo Florio concluded that the process 'had more modest effects on efficiency than the theory of property rights and other orthodox privatization theories may have expected. On the other hand, privatization did have substantial regressive effects on the distribution of incomes and wealth in the United Kingdom.'[25] The removal of cross subsidies and the introduction of new pricing structures increased the costs of electricity, gas, water and public transport for some low-income consumers including 'a substantial share of the aged, the disabled, children of single parents, the long-term unemployed, and the working poor'.[26] Florio estimates that a million low-income households in Britain ended up worse off as a result of privatization.

Where state institutions couldn't be sold off to private investors wholesale, functions previously in the state sector could be contracted out to private companies. From a mid-'70s peak of 750,000, the number of civil servants had fallen below 500,000 by the mid-'90s, largely as a result of this process. Beneath the rhetoric, the state did not so much shrink as become more efficient in transferring tax revenues to private corporations. And the political supporters of this rejection of the public service ethos thought that the state employees who remained could be made to behave more efficiently by the introduction of a market-like system of rewards and punishments. A series of initiatives sought to strip out the old flummery about the common good and import competition and incentives into state administration.[27] Personnel from private industry came into the civil service to enforce this new regime of internal markets, targets, performance-related pay and management. This amounted to a profound transformation of the state sector as the ethos of disinterested public service in the context of stable careers gave way to what Michael Sandel later called 'market-mimicking governance' in an atmosphere of growing insecurity.[28]

Already weakened by the sale of state-owned industries, the trade unions suffered further from wholesale changes in the laws governing the private sector. As Will Hutton explained in his book *The State We're In*, the legislation introduced by Thatcher and her successor John Major 'transformed British industrial relations' and created the framework for 'easily the most aggressive assault on British unions' in the twentieth century.[29] Changes to the law were complemented by steep rises in unemployment in heavily unionized sectors. A severe recession in the early 1980s left organized labour demoralized and ever less able to defend the interests of workers in a world being reordered in the interests of capital. By 2000 a Labour Prime Minister happily acknowledged that his country had 'the most restrictive trade union laws in the western world'.[30]

The destruction of trade union power was at the heart of the Thatcher project from the outset. In a series of papers published between 1976 and 1978, John Hoskyns, the future head of the Downing Street Policy Unit, insisted that national recovery would require a 'sea-change in Britain's political economy'. He had no doubt that the unions would have to be destroyed: 'there is one major obstacle – the negative role of the trade unions'. Other steps were necessary, according to Hoskyns, including a period of 'sustained monetary discipline, balanced budgets, public sector wage restraint'.[31] The tax burden would need to be shifted away from income and onto expenditure, the private sector would need to be deregulated and the revenues from North Sea oil would need to be used to cut government borrowing.[32] But curbing trade union power was central; only then would the wealthy feel sufficiently confident to invest in new industry. In March 1979 the Conservative Shadow Cabinet accepted Hoskyns' recommendations for economic renewal and the neoliberal experiment began in earnest.[33]

A little later, in the United States, President Reagan moved quickly to establish the tone of his new administration – he fired thirteen thousand striking air traffic controllers and moved to defang existing legislation designed to protect workers. Faced with a hostile Congress, Reagan appointed vehement critics of the unions to the Labor Department and the National Labor Relations Board, the body charged with settling complaints against employers. Employers took the hint and illegally fired workers who showed signs of militancy, expanded the use of temporary workers and began the process of 'offshoring', where factories were relocated in countries with lower wages.[34] Union membership declined steeply as income inequality grew.

The private sector in the US had long maintained a powerful hold on state expenditure through its management of weapons research and production in a permanent war economy. Indeed the military-industrial systems in both the US and the UK – within which individuals traced lucrative circles through government employment, lobbying and corporate management – provided the prototype for the more extensive restructuring of the state along lines amenable to private investors. After Reagan's victory the military establishment expanded considerably as the general population paid contractors to refurbish Second World War battleships and cook up hallucinatory boondoggles like the Strategic Defense Initiative. The Bush II administration went on to expand the dynamics of military procurement by using private military contractors on an unprecedented scale and by creating a homeland security apparatus that would then pour money down the throats of retired and serving intelligence operatives, political imagineers and well-connected operators in the Bush-Cheney milieu.[35]

The eventual return of nominally social democratic or liberal governments in Britain and the United States brought no respite. The New Democrats enthusiastically embraced the idea that the state should adopt market mechanisms. In a widely influential book, *Reinventing Government: How the Entrepreneurial Spirit is Transforming the Public Sector*, David Osborne and Ted Gaebler argued that 'entre-preneurial leaders' should concentrate on finding pragmatic ways to make government more efficient. Indeed they gloried 'in blur-ring the distinction between the public and the private'.[36] Clinton heartily endorsed their message, declaring that 'this book gives us the blueprint'.[37] Similarly, Al Gore's objective in the 1993 Report of the National Performance Review was 'to make government customer friendly'.[38] The coordination between Wall Street and the administration reached new heights in the period after the Cold War as financiers worked in the US Treasury department presided over a speculative boom in the technology sector at home and sought to prise open capital markets abroad, in Asia in particular. And today, now that the banks have soaked up unprecedented state subsidies, the NGO Public Citizen reports that at least 70 former legislators are working for finance companies in an effort to forestall or minimize regulation by the Obama administration.[39]

The centre left on the other side of the Atlantic had, like the Democrats, declared itself New. In government, inspired in part by Clinton's successful re-election campaign in 1996, New Labour also seized on the language of market efficiency. By the time they arrived in office it had already 'become commonplace to speak of a change from public administration to public management'.[40] The incoming government seized on the trend with puppyish enthusiasm and in 1998 it published an 'annual report' that imitated those of large companies. In it Prime Minister Blair explained that chang-ing a government was 'like sweeping away the entire management of a company'. Government would have to change to satisfy a more demanding electorate: 'in all walks of life, people act as consum-ers, not just citizens'.[41] By 1999, in a speech attempting to express support for the public sector, Blair was to be heard telling civil servants that they were 'social entrepreneurs'.[42]

New Labour spent huge sums on private contractors. By 2007 the state was passing £68 billion to private sector companies, some 20 per cent of current expenditure.[43] In 2006 it had spent £2 billion on management consultants alone.[44] It drafted businessmen and women into government and into the civil service. The state turned to private investors to fund the building of new hospitals and schools, which the government then leased. By 2009 the government had signed more than 900 private finance contracts for assets worth £72 billion.[45]

The collective provision of social goods such as education and health, never fully achieved, gave way to an allegedly pragmatic or post-ideological programme of fragmentation and commodification. In purely commercial terms the entrepreneurial state proved disastrously inept. The same state that had presided over the invention of the computer contrived to hand billions of pounds to information technology companies that delivered late or not at all. The private finance initiatives proved amazingly lucrative for their backers. This interpenetration of the state and the private sectors culminated in so-called 'Public Private Partnerships' in which the responsibilities and functions of civil servants and private corporations inevitably became confused. By the time the state began spending further billions to save the financial sector from its own folly, the dysfunctional relationship between the state and the private sector had long since turned flagrantly abusive.

While the penalties for dissidence grew sharper, the rewards for accommodation could be very sweet. The management of the companies Thatcher privatized saw their pay increase by as much as 600 per cent.[46] At times the new emphasis on market mechanisms approached parody as politicians came to sound like excited graduate trainees in detergents companies:

> It has been the job of New Labour's architects to translate their understanding of the customer into offerings he or she is willing to pay for. And then, and only then, to convey to potential customers the attributes of that offering through all the different components that make up a successful brand – product positioning, packaging, advertising and communications.[47]

The population as a whole had little or no opportunity to shape the rules that governed national economies, much less the structure of the global system; instead citizens were encouraged to express themselves through consumption. At election time this privately oriented population was on hand to provide legitimacy and psychological reassurance for managerial elites. Professional politicians concentrated on giving the financial markets what they wanted and on reconciling the population to the consequences. They became spokesman for the spirit of the age, experts on the unavoidable implications of new technology, curators of necessity, all the while ignoring that 'the only direct, efficient forces in history are human motives'.[48] Once they had reconciled the wider population to the pattern of action and inaction that the business class wanted they could count themselves successful and indulge guiltlessly in a plutocratic style of life.

Just as private capital increased its control of the agenda and the management of the state, market relations also came to exert greater influence over the family and the realm of intimate relations. In the absence of state intervention, individuals resorted as best they could to the market to make up for deficiencies in social provision. Christopher Lasch noted how 'the hope that political action' would 'gradually improve society' had 'given way to a determination to survive the general wreckage or, more modestly, to hold one's life together in the face of mounting pressures'.[49] In conditions of steepening inequality and sharpening social competition, a revival of 'Victorian' social conservatism coincided with rapid growth in the markets for illegal and legal psychoactive drugs, as well as prostitution and gambling. Social breakdown and the distress associated with it provided lucrative opportunities for established businesses, criminals and conservative political entrepreneurs alike.

The education and health sectors in Britain struggled to maintain the qualified insulation from market forces they had enjoyed in the previous era. A management culture borrowed from the private sector that used permanent audit to seek efficiency gains and that purported to serve the interests of citizen-consumers placed public sector workers under a new and demoralizing surveillance. Meanwhile universities in need of funds had little choice but to accept corporate money. As social status and career success correlated ever more closely with service to profit-making entities, many academics were willing to play along. A Labour Education Secretary, Charles Clarke, channelled the spirit of the age when he claimed that the idea of education for its own sake was 'a little bit dodgy'; students, he insisted, needed 'a relationship with the workplace'.[50] This insistence that market values can be applied to education continues to inform both policy and rhetoric. In November 2009 the irrepressible Peter Mandelson was promising a 'consumer revolution' in higher education.[51]

To a large extent the investing classes, usually described in abstract terms as 'the market' or 'market forces', constituted the effectual public in both countries. In 2008 David Rothkopf noted with only mild concern that there are 'a group of a few thousand people among the corporate elite who effectively control perhaps $100 trillion, two thirds of the world's total assets'.[52] These few thousand people moved away from the reality of the world they controlled and created hermetic environments where they could enjoy unspoiled nature and the company of their peers. At the World Economic Forum in Davos and elsewhere they met and developed a common response to matters of common concern. Perhaps the most telling change has been their withdrawal from the shared life of taxation into a parallel world of offshore privilege.

While politicians competed to secure the support of this corporate elite, the fact of their massive material power vanished as a matter of general consideration, as civil society and the fields of publicity became filled with a vivid but vapid cultural pluralism. Even so, the media proved as susceptible as ever to the stories and spectacles that surround and dignify the controllers of great wealth.

If politicians and journalists allowed themselves to be won over, the servants of the state it seems also served this elite Anglo-American public out of settled conviction: In a rare moment of off-the-record candour, one intelligence official explained to the historian Bernard Porter that 'the Anglo-Saxon model of capitalism' remains on 'MI5's list of potential targets to be safeguarded against subversion'.[53]

The commitment of the US and UK states to Anglo-Saxon capitalism found theoretical support from the prevailing intellectual culture. One widely praised book argued that the world's 'constitutional order' was in the process of transforming itself from an order of nation-states to one of market-states. In 2002, in *The Shield of Achilles*, the constitutional lawyer Philip Bobbitt explained that the market-state was an 'emerging constitutional order that promises to maximize the opportunity of its people, tending to privatize many state activities and making government more responsive to the market'.[54] Over more than 900 pages Bobbitt sought to demonstrate the historical inevitability of the state's retreat from welfare provision and the increasing power of market forces to determine state action. Those countries that adopted the market-friendly policies of Clinton and Blair would, according to Bobbitt, gain a 'decisive advantage' over their rivals.[55]

Changes in the structure of the global economy further entrenched the advantages enjoyed by this reinvigorated neoliberal public. As the Bretton Woods system collapsed, national governments found it increasingly difficult to ignore the demands of international investors. Walter Wriston summed up the consensus among those who controlled the global economy when he mixed the language of finance and democracy:

> In international financial markets today, a vote on the soundness of each country's fiscal and monetary policies, in comparison with those of every other country in the world, is held in the trading rooms of the world every minute of the day . . . This continuing

direct plebiscite on the value of currencies and commodities proceeds by methods that are growing more sophisticated every day.[56]

In this way, private investors centred in Wall Street and the City of London determined the limits of state action in much of the world, performing a permanent audit of government policy. In the United States, business had long had a preponderant role in establishing the bounds of political debate through its financial backing for both Republican and Democratic candidates. In the years after 1980, business control of the technocratic basis of policy-making became ever more complete, particularly when it came to the regulation of the financial sector. In a sympathetic account of the Federal Reserve published in the early 1990s, David M. Jones noted that:

> Modern Fed Chairmen are chosen, in effect, by the financial markets. The political process is secondary. Typically, the White House leaks to the press a list of potential nominees for the top job at the US central bank and leaves the choice largely to the collective choice of the financial markets.[57]

If the key players in the financial markets had considerable influence over the choice of appointments and the details of policy, their ability to prevent discussion of their own domestic and foreign power sometimes seemed even greater. Still, every now and again traces of reality came to light, sometimes in the most unlikely places.

In the acknowledgements section to *The Lexus and the Olive Tree*, one of the most enthusiastic accounts of globalization, Thomas Friedman thanks a number of people for their help with the book, including Federal Reserve Chairman Alan Greenspan, former Treasury Secretary Robert Rubin, a hedge fund manager and a bond trader. Friedman then goes on to thank some people 'from the private sector'. The bond trader, the hedge fund manager, and

Robert Rubin, by then an employee of Citigroup, were somehow in the public sector as far as Friedman was concerned.[58] One can read a great deal by Thomas Friedman while remaining none the wiser, but this is a moment of true illumination.

The idea that the effectually public status of finance might imply certain responsibilities did occasionally surface. In 2005, Martin Wolf noted in the context of the Asian crises of the late 1990s that:

> The management of any systematically important bank that has to be rescued by the state should be disbarred, as a matter of course, from further work in the financial industry . . . Managers are, in an important sense, public servants. If they abuse that trust, they should be treated accordingly.[59]

But while this sort of talk might have enlivened debate when the irresponsibility and cronyism was located in Asia, the period before 2007 rarely saw similar reservations expressed about Anglo-Saxon practices. Finance and the rest of the business class insisted that public benefits flowed directly from their blameless private ambitions. The media praised their dynamism while ignoring their reliance on a state-coordinated system of credit. Though challenged in the last years of the twentieth century by the so-called anti-globalization movement, these effectual neoliberal publics continued to dominate the economy, the political process and the climate of opinion. It is to the wider consequences of their continuing domination of political and economic life in Britain and the United States that we now turn.

PART 2

The Public in Eclipse

CHAPTER SIX

The Outlines of the Crisis

IT IS A commonplace to announce that we are in the midst of a crisis. This can be glossed in any number of ways – we face social, financial, fiscal, environmental and political crises. The media face their own crisis as they struggle to remain both plausible and solvent. But underlying all these crises, and to a considerable extent shaping them, is a crisis of publicity. By this I mean that the population cannot currently secure and share the information required for independent political action. The public, in the sense of an informed and autonomous body capable of initiating policy and changing legislation, exists, but it does not include the overwhelming majority of us. In the neoliberal settlement, public status belongs securely only to those who embody the logic of acquisition by force, fraud and free exchange. The public conceived as a body qualified by the possession of citizenship to determine the content of politics and to restrain elites does not exist. The constitution of knowledge leaves most people incapable of establishing an accurate account of the world and sharing that account with others.

We have been deprived of the knowledge necessary for self-government and political agency in three crucial respects. We lack knowledge about the world beyond our direct experience. For example, we have yet to register fully the power of money to shape the constitution of representations on which we rely when we come to engage with one another and with our governing institutions. More generally, vast swathes of state-corporate activity remain unreported in detail and barely acknowledged in outline, until they erupt into general awareness as the disaster of war or economic crisis. We lack relevant knowledge about our fellow citizens, even though the population as a whole is subject to something like permanent surveillance by the polling industry.

Finally we lack knowledge of the conditions that need to be in place if we are to lead lives that are in some substantive sense freely chosen. The presently governing ideology describes human nature in radically misleading and degrading terms. The marinade of sociobiology and neoliberalism in which we live and construct our self-understanding confirms and secures the current system. We are estranged from our own needs and capabilities, from each other, and from the world, by a radically unreliable system of information.

This crisis – our crisis – has been a long time in the making. It was visible to Dewey and Lippmann in America in the 1920s and, despite the popular achievements of the New Deal in the US and the Labour government in Britain, the effective exclusion of the majority from decisions about matters of common concern gathered pace after the Second World War as the population came to rely on bureaucratically organized groups to defend its interests. Popular mobilization and militancy in the 1930s and 1940s gave way to the culture of liberal administration. The labour movement in the United States accepted the place assigned to it in the mixed economy, thanks in part to an aggressive propaganda campaign by private business to fend off further threats to its pre-eminence and thanks to a move by the state to associate efforts to democratize the economy with Soviet communism. Though chafing under regulation, and committed to generous benefits for employees, corporate business remained substantially intact. In Britain the post-war settlement seemed to give the leaders of the unions a permanent place in the national structure of power, so long as they accepted the existing systems of ownership and control. State action in both countries hampered efforts to maintain and expand programmes to institute structural change, by associating radicalism with Stalinism, and by drawing the leadership of the unions into collaboration against Cold War enemies.

Both state activism and the operations of the market steadily undermined popular representation in the post-war settlement. In America on the one hand the state arrested or harassed radicals, on the other it redistributed wealth and regulated industry and so encouraged the sense that radical change was unnecessary. In Britain the ability of the organized working class to communicate declined when commercial pressures forced the trade union movement to give up its newspaper, the *Daily Herald*. Before its transformation into the *Sun* and its sale to Rupert Murdoch, the *Herald* had retained a large and devoted readership. But lack of advertising revenues eventually made it impossible for the labour movement to maintain a large-scale publishing capability.[1]

As noted in Chapter 5, public servants worked with elites from labour and private industry to determine policy. Instead of translating popular demands for reform into legislation, they implemented solutions from above. In the United States, Johnson's Great Society programme attempted to engineer away the problems of poverty by bringing in technocratic expertise from the universities. In Britain, the Labour government at the same time tried to break the power of the Treasury and to remake economic governance in ways that would serve promote industrial development and demote finance. But it did so in the absence of a widely debated and understood programme of social transformation. When in the 1970s business moved to break with the social democratic settlement established after 1945, the informed and assertive mass movements that had secured that settlement – the labour movement above all – could not defend it.

The new political order of 1979–80 led to a pervasive confusion of the public and the private. Politicians sought electoral success by marketing their personalities, and a sophisticated perception-management industry did what it could to transform claims about the private qualities of politicians into qualifications for public office.

Campaigns repeatedly focused on issues of personal competence and character and exploited the emotional resources of race and sexuality. The facts of biography substituted for programme. In the United States the presidency has been dominated since 1981 by figures who have shared an ability to create the illusion of intimate engagement with a mass audience. The three two-term presidents, Reagan, Clinton and Bush II, were in their different ways monsters of affability.

Immediately after the terrorist attacks of September 2001, President Bush announced that the country was at war. Those who asked what they could do for their country during this new emergency were told to stay positive and to cooperate with the authorities.[2] Private gestures – hugging, praying and shopping – were offered as a substitute for political participation. The American people were not expected to discuss what the attacks meant, how their state should respond, let alone the constitutionality of a President declaring war. Reading the rhetoric of the Bush administration, and of his war without geographical or temporal limits, it is hard to forgive Lippmann's faith that insiders would create an accurate picture of the world in the minds of the population. When it was not generating hysteria by talking up the threat of nuclear terrorism the Bush administration produced a steady succession of comforting or reassuring stereotypes, through which the population were discouraged from seeing the state's actions in anything other than the bright colours of moralistic sentimentality. The black and white of public deliberation was, wherever possible, denounced as defeatism.

Of course, what Richard Sennett in *The Fall of Public Man* calls 'the superimposition of private upon public imagery'[3] is a long-standing feature of electoral politics. Writing in the late 1970s, Sennett saw Nixon as the latest in a long line of right-wing populists:

> On the one side there is someone against the Establishment who dramatizes his motivations rather than his acts; he is contemptuous of the Establishment, whose feelings are hollow because always

shielded by decorum and pretension. On the other hand, this mythical Establishment of persons act contemptuously towards the little man, but they don't deserve their self-assurance: further they are in conspiracy, somehow, with the scum that wants to tear apart the whole society.[4]

Sennett here describes the politics of social resentment that will later secure two-term presidencies for both Reagan and the younger Bush and that has already lent Sarah Palin a national significance. In each case the drama of personality triumphs over the pallid world of fact. The spokesman for General Electric becomes the champion of individual enterprise; the wealthy and work-shy scion of a patrician New England family becomes the straight-talking, brush-clearing Texan; the avid promoter of corporate urban development becomes the embodiment of an emotionally potent 'real America'.

Similarly, both the political class and those responsible for reporting them have always tended to prefer the intricacies of personal animosity and the microscopic frame of scandal to the substance of policy; socially astute men and women in Anglo-America take care not to seem too concerned with matters of principle, lest their peers worry that they will not respect the calculus of favours given and received. Writing in 1958, the American journalist James Reston remarked sardonically that 'the Capital is in its glory tonight': 'After being bored to death with the economic crisis of the Western World it finally has the kind of simple political personal conflict it likes: a partisan conflict about who paid Sherman Adams' hotel bill in Boston.'[5]

What has changed is the extent to which coverage of the political process in general and of Presidential elections in particular now appears devoid of anything but the language of the private sphere. It may be a cliché of left-wing complaint that political candidates are now marketed like brands, but those who manage these brands talk openly about the work they do. Senator John McCain's campaign manager Rick Davis was happy to admit that 'this election is not about issues; this election is about a composite view of what people take away from these candidates',[6] while Desirée Rogers, the White House's Social Secretary, boasted that 'we have the best brand on earth: the Obama brand. Our possibilities are endless'.[7] Sure enough, two months later in June 2009, the Obama campaign picked up two awards at the Cannes Lion International Advertising Festival.[8] Political differences remain, and they are sometimes highly significant in terms of their impact on the general population, but they are nigh-on impossible to discern in mainstream descriptions of the parties or in the utterances of the candidates.

Marketing techniques have been used to promote the ideas and background beliefs against which individual politicians build their brands. The simple slogans and emotionally charged images of commercial advertising dovetail with state of the art opinion- and perception-management. Academics, media executives and psychological-warfare specialists have collaborated in a series of product launches in which insubstantial concepts like 'The End of History', 'The War on Terror' and 'Operation Iraqi Freedom' have been given an air of solidity by the astute expenditure of money. And over-arching these capitalized phrases, industry and finance have lavished billions of dollars to promote the free market principles that in turn justified the capture of the American state by corporate and financial elites.

Politicians remain attentive to the general population, certainly, but they measure their success in terms of the extent to which they are able to defuse or re-direct popular passions. Politicians inquire into public attitudes in order to discover how a winning electoral proposition might be formulated, or how to fine-tune their communications over the course of a term in office. This reinvention of politics as a series of product launches supported by market research took place within a consensus about the related fields of political economy and foreign policy – competition between political parties increasingly becomes a matter of brand positioning, a politics of sentiment, symbolism and identity.

In the UK, Tony Blair offered a glimpse of politics in this madcap new normality in a memo written in 2000, as his government struggled to deal with 'a clutch of issues' including the controversy caused when a Norfolk farmer shot and killed a burglar in his house. Blair complained about 'the lack of any response from us that appeared to empathize with public concern and then channel it into the correct course'. Blair wanted to show the British people that he was on their side and 'standing up for Britain'. Accordingly he called for 'two or three eye-catching initiatives' that were 'entirely conventional in terms of their attitude to the family'.[9] In other words, policies were to be crafted to serve a communications agenda. And it could hardly be otherwise. Market forces were placing an ever-greater strain on British households; all the more reason for the government to advertise their 'entirely conventional' attitude to the family. The government should *appear* to empathize with public concern, *the better to channel it into the correct course*. Bernays would have loved Blair's unselfconscious use of the language of hydraulic engineering.

Meanwhile business insisted on its right to a selectively public status. The advocates of 'corporate social responsibility' and 'corporate citizenship' demanded that corporations be treated as reliable stewards of the public good, even though they were bound by law to serve only their shareholders' interests and were often run in practice for the benefit of senior managers and their financial advisors. In some respects, those who spoke for the corporations had a point. Just after the First World War the German statesman and industrialist Walter Rathenau noted that:

> The claims of ownership are subdivided in such a fashion, and are so mobile, that the enterprise assumes an independent life, as if it belongs to no one; it takes an objective existence, such as in earlier days was embodied only in state and church, in a municipal

corporation, in the life of a guild or religious order. The deperson-
alization of the enterprise, the detachment of property from the
possessor, leads to a point where the enterprise becomes transformed into an institution which resembles the state in character.[10]

Though their representatives alternately insist on their public right to
citizenship and their private right to be left alone, they have more in
common with states than with human beings. Indeed these state-like
entities have become partners in government through outsourcing
and their capabilities have enhanced the state's ability to project
power. In 1983 the National Security Council designated 'the nation's
domestic and international telecommunications resources, including
commercial, private and government-owned' as 'essential elements
in support of US national security policy and strategy'.[11] The state
uses these corporate telecommunications resources to gather intelligence and conduct diplomacy. This includes 'public diplomacy',
the polite term for psychological warfare when it is conducted by
a state against its own and foreign populations. Those who complain
about US cultural imperialism are often derided for simple-minded
anti-Americanism. In light of the National Security Council's own
remarks on the strategic value of private telecommunications companies, this criticism seems somewhat more simple-minded.

Pretensions to a public status, whether justified by service to
the state or by notions like corporate citizenship, do not imply any
dilution of private control. Having toyed with the idea of allowing
employees some say in managing companies, Labour backed down
the moment they learnt that 'the big end of town' didn't like the idea.
Geoff Mulgan told the academic Shann Turnbull that 'company directors were concerned that they would be made accountable to people
other than shareholders and institutional investors were frightened
that it would destroy shareholder value'.[12]

Adding to this confusion of the public and the private the media
insisted on their right to treat intimate life as a commercial resource.

Journalists justified their pursuit of salacious stories as a way of enforcing public norms of morality. One prominent newspaper editor even claimed that scandal lured the masses to their coverage of 'public affairs'. In an eloquently timed speech – it was delivered nine-and-a-half weeks after the collapse of Lehmans – Paul Dacre of the *Daily Mail* insisted on his right to shame individuals who he felt had somehow failed to measure up to acceptable standards of behaviour:

> For hundreds of years, the press has played a role in [public shaming]. It has the freedom to identify those who have offended public standards of decency – the very standards its readers believe in – and hold the transgressors up to public condemnation. If their readers don't agree with the defence of such values, they would not buy those papers in such huge numbers.
>
> Put another way, if mass-circulation newspapers, which also devote considerable space to reporting and analysis of public affairs, don't have the freedom to write about scandal, I doubt whether they will retain their mass circulations with the obvious worrying implications for the democratic process.[13]

Intimate life, as scandal or as human interest, has always been the stuff of popular journalism. The selective use of the media to make public the details of private life provides newspaper owners in particular with enormous power. Celebrity provides a steady source of revenue, which can then be used to subsidize 'reporting and analysis of public affairs' that focuses on the amiability and competence of politicians of whom the proprietor approves and on the immorality or instability of everyone else. Seen in this light the large media operations come to resemble a system of explicit patronage and implicit blackmail more than a means of providing the majority with the information that they need for active citizenship. In other words, when the gigantic intimacies of the famous don't displace the discussion of public affairs entirely, the categories of private life dominate the description of both politics and the economy.

Likewise, while the institutions of the private economy aspire to the condition of citizenship, they also urge citizens to reinvent themselves on commercial lines. Personality, looks and talent became ever more efficiently commodified. Back in the early 1950s, C. Wright Mills had noted how 'in many strata of white-collar employment, such traits as courtesy, helpfulness, and kindness, once intimate, are now part of the impersonal means of livelihood'.[14] Now the workplace demands an ever more convincing display of enthusiasm and even affection from employees. The corporation seeks to integrate itself into the structure of state administration on the one hand and the emotional lives of its employees and customers on the other. Those employees and customers – the majority of the population – are denied knowledge of the impersonal systems on which they rely and are offered instead a series of misleading impressions and the imitation of human concern.

CHAPTER SEVEN

Estranged From the World

Incompetence and aimlessness, corruption and disloyalty, panic and ultimate disaster, must come to any people which is denied assured access to the facts.

Walter Lippmann

W HEN WE TRY to understand the world most of us have to rely on information that is profoundly unsafe. The coverage that preceded the invasion of Iraq in 2003 and the breakdown of the financial system in 2007–8 demonstrated the systemic unreliability of the media system on which we depend. These failures of reporting are not anomalous; they are predictable features of the current system of communication. They should leave us in no doubt of the need for radical change in the structure of the media. It is not enough for journalists to declare that lessons have been learnt and that they will be less credulous in the future. The media must be reformed.

In 2002–3 the British and American states secured consent or compliance for war by immersing their populations in an overlapping set of untruths. Their success depended on a highly centralized media system that delivered their claims to mass audiences without serious scrutiny. The population as a whole had few, if any, means to challenge the claims being made in ways that would achieve publicity. Popular opposition could not translate into political action since the two main parties in both countries supported the war. And the state ran riot through the institutions of civil society, both openly and covertly. Retired generals appeared as accredited experts on network news, and journalists who were wittingly or unwittingly working for the intelligence services dominated the pre-war analysis. The mystique of secret intelligence and the prestige of state-recognized expertise drove dissenting opinions to the margins.

The case for war set out to domestic audiences largely rested on two kinds of false claims. First, the US and UK governments stated baldly that Saddam Hussein still maintained an arsenal of weapons of mass destruction. Second, they insinuated that that his regime was responsible for the attacks on New York and Washington in September 2001. The administrations of the two countries deliberately treated unsubstantiated claims by defectors and ambiguous satellite data as incontrovertible proof of an active WMD capability. In doing so they contradicted the much more cautious assessments of their own intelligence analysts. Key administration officials repeatedly insisted that the existence of weapons of mass destruction had been established beyond any doubt. Vice President Cheney was no more categorical than most administration officials when he claimed that, 'simply stated, there is no doubt that Saddam Hussein now has weapons of mass destruction'.[1] Prime Minister Blair ridiculed those who expressed doubts: 'we are asked now seriously to accept that . . . Saddam decided unilaterally to destroy those weapons. I say that such a claim is palpably absurd.'[2] As well as distorting and exaggerating the evidence it appears that the two states fabricated evidence outright. The claim that Iraq was seeking to buy uranium from Niger, for example, derived from forged documentation that might have been the work of the secret service of one or other country or of the secret service of an ally.[3] There was no evidence at all for claims that Iraq had been complicit in the 9/11 attacks, though this did not hinder the Bush administration in its efforts to persuade millions of citizens of a fantastical conspiracy theory. The scale of the mendacity of the British and American administrations even now remains shocking. Charles Lewis and Mark Reading Smith of the Center for Public

Integrity in the US have counted more than 900 false claims made by the President and seven key administration figures concerning the status of Saddam Hussein's weapons programmes and his links to al Qaeda.[4]

States lie to secure their objectives and often their most effective advocates believe wholeheartedly in claims that other members of the official apparatus know full well to be untrue. Indeed, the virtuosity of the state resides in its ability to use true and false claims, sincerity and deception, in a communications repertoire that also includes bribery and both retail and wholesale terror. As Friedrich Nietzsche put it, 'the state never has any use for truth as such, but only for truth which is useful to it, more precisely for anything whatever useful to it whether it be truth, half-truth or error'.[5] The current media cannot register the nature of the state in this respect and their unshakeable naïveté in the face of official claims derives from their structural dependence on it. Their failure to challenge state mendacity is as predictable as the mendacity itself. And while in the years that followed the press has focused endlessly whether Bush and Blair were sincere this is to miss the point. It was their job to believe what they claimed to believe.

Whether individuals were consciously lying when they warned about the danger from Iraq's weapons of mass destruction matters less than the conduct of the media in reporting their claims. One need only note what was happening in the media from the summer of 2002 onwards to register the degree to which reporting diverged from reality. A senior British official wrote in July 2002 that in the United States 'the intelligence and facts were being fixed' around military action that 'was now seen as inevitable'.[6] Had any journalist claimed that summer that the US administration considered war inevitable and that they were fixing the intelligence accordingly they would have been denounced as a hopeless paranoiac. Instead in the run-up to the war the media accepted and amplified official claims about the status of Iraq's weapons programme and about the links between Saddam Hussein and the 9/11 attacks. Some of the impact of their coverage can be traced in polling data. In 2001 only 3 per cent of Americans mentioned Saddam Hussein or Iraq as possible instigators of the terrorist attacks on New York and Washington. By the summer of 2003 a *Washington Post* poll showed that nearly 70 per cent of those asked thought that Saddam Hussein was personally involved.[7]

A number of publications subsequently admitted to errors in their coverage in terms that amount to something like a cover-up. In May 2004 the *New York Times* acknowledged that they had found 'a number of instances of coverage that was not as rigorous as it should have been'. This, they claimed, was because the paper's editors and journalists 'sometimes fell for misinformation' from Iraqi exiles. The authors of the piece go on to say that they have been re-examining 'the failings of American and allied intelligence', and 'allegations of official gullibility and hype'. So the newspaper and the government both made the mistake of trusting some wily orientals; the intelligence agencies were guilty of unspecified lapses from their usual high standards of conduct; and the government overstated its case. The possibility that the US and allied intelligence agencies might have been brilliantly successful in securing domestic support for a war of aggression does not feature in their soul-searching. That gullibility and hype might not be the worst of the administration's sins also fails to register, even as the paper assures its readers that they will continue with 'aggressive' reporting on the issue of weapons of mass destruction.[8]

This particular collapse of reporting standards in the run-up to the war took place over quite a short period, from the White House's product launch in September 2002 until the invasion in March of the following year. But the media have failed to provide an accurate account of the domestic and the global economy for at least 30 years. This chronic failure had its origins in the reorganization of the state and of the governing orthodoxy begun by Thatcher and

Reagan. Over the last generation the major political parties in both Britain and the United States gave up on the idea that the public or common interest can be asserted in the face of demands for the liberalization of markets. Individual self-interest sufficed to stabilize the financial system and those who ran the state had to resign themselves to managing, rather than changing, the economic and political system. In this environment competence came close to supplanting programme altogether in electoral politics. Everyone – everyone who wasn't one of Henry Fielding's nobodies – agreed on the fundamentals of economic policy; voters just had to decide which team of managers to put in place. As early as 1988, Democratic presidential hopeful Michael Dukakis was insisting that 'this election isn't about ideology, it's about competence'.[9] The more the programmes of the major parties converged, the greater the emphasis on novelty; the New Democrats and New Labour successfully repackaged Thatcher and Reagan's policies using the second oldest trick in the marketers' book.

Once the major parties embraced the main assumptions of the neoliberal settlement, descriptions of the economy that had little or no factual basis achieved widespread – in political terms, universal – assent. As Paul Krugman has noted: 'a handful of wealthy cranks can support an impressive-looking array of think tanks, research institutes, foundations, and so on devoted to promoting an economic doctrine they like'.[10] When a very large number of wealthy cranks together controlled much of the media and the state apparatus, the results were even more impressive. Myths about the economy concocted privately became the basis for what passed for public debate, and only those who committed themselves energetically and intelligently to these fantasies were permitted access to the commanding heights of the governing institutions. Al Hubbard, one of the two people asked to draw up a list of candidates for the job of replacing Alan Greenspan as chairman of the Federal Reserve, liked Ben Bernanke's people skills, but he was just as impressed by his doctrinal orthodoxy: 'we were impressed with his theories of the world and the way he thinks. He believes in free markets.'[11]

This faith in free markets and its accompanying theology of regulatory torpor became requirements for expert status, and hence for reliable access to publicity. Only those who accepted the crackpot contradictions of *laissez-faire* under conditions of corporate oligopoly were permitted into positions of authority in the United States, Britain and in the World Bank and the International Monetary Fund. The dogma had to be repeated with every appearance of sincerity; the state could not presume to set limits to the operations of markets; market forces would, if left unfettered, deliver growth and prosperity for all. Over the course of a generation, economic policy became the ever more exclusive preserve of tough-minded and self-confident fantasists.

This was a crisis years in the making. It was entirely predictable and indeed was predicted, albeit by figures who for the most part remained marginal. For decades Marxist economists had pointed out that long-term rates of economic growth were steadily declining and that what growth there was depended on increasing levels of debt. As inequality increased and median incomes stagnated most people could only spend more if they borrowed more. Since economic growth remained sluggish investors turned to financial speculation to generate higher returns.[12] By 1999 the British economist Peter Warburton was warning that 'the credit and capital markets have grown too rapidly, with too little transparency and accountability. Prepare for an explosion that will rock the roots of the western financial system to its foundations.'[13] In 2006 Ann Pettifor published *The Coming First World Debt Crisis*, in which she pointed out that the rising levels of debt and speculation could not be sustained indefinitely.[14] In the same year the fund manager Peter Schiff was warning anyone who would listen that they were facing 'the mother of all bubbles'.[15] Disaster seemed so inevitable to the cleverest speculators by then that John Paulson and others were trying to figure out ways of making money out of it.

Yet policy-makers remained weirdly calm. In 2005 Timothy Geithner, Barack Obama's future Treasury Secretary, had assured the financial markets that there was 'no sign of a large, macroeconomic shock on the horizon'.[16] As late as February 2007 Bernanke assured Congress that problems in the sub-prime mortgage sector weren't 'a broad financial concern or a major factor in assessing the course of the economy'.[17] Similarly, long into 2007 the major business media remained relaxed to the point of sedation, even as banks began to warn of rapid deterioration in the US housing market.[18] Again in February an article in the *Financial Times* complained that one UK lender, the Alliance & Leicester, had 'taken an overly cautious view of the mortgage market'.[19] And in May 2007 the paper was telling its readers that 'only the UK's top 15 or 20 companies' were safe from acquisition by private equity partnerships buoyed by apparently limitless cheap credit.[20]

The head of the Confederation of British Industry, Richard Lambert, himself a former editor of the *Financial Times*, was later moved to acknowledge that 'precious few journalists gave any hints at all of what was to come'.[21] In fact, far from giving a hint of what was in store, the media enthusiastically publicized the claims of those who saw no end to the rise in asset prices. The chief economist at the National Association of Realtors, David Lereah, author of *Why the Real Estate Boom Will Not Bust* (2005), was cited in the major media more than 1,700 times in the two years before the housing bubble burst, more than three times more often than any other source.[22]

The failures of the major media over Iraq and the state of the global economy are only the most obvious examples of a much larger ongoing failure to describe reality. They are not unrepresentative deviations from an otherwise adequate system of representation. The scrambling of the public and the private in the Anglo-American media contributes to this ongoing failure by shrouding the connections between decision-makers in effective secrecy while publicizing the intimate affairs of private individuals. In August 2008 the assistant bureau chief of the Associated Press in Los Angeles summed up the prevailing judgement of the major news media when he wrote that 'now and for the foreseeable future, virtually everything involving Britney is a big deal'.[23]

Meanwhile, the Bilderberg group of American and European business and political elites insists that its meetings are not secret but that they are 'private', and the media show an almost courtly sensitivity to the Bilderbergers' right to conduct their business away from the glare of publicity. This refusal to treat these annual meetings as a big deal is especially surprising when compared with the media's fearless curiosity about a succession of celebrities who seem less able to influence the global agenda. An archive search indicates that the Associated Press, or 'the essential global news network' as it likes to call itself, has included the word Bilderberg in five articles since 1998. The phrase 'Trilateral Commission' appeared 15 times over the same period. The words 'Bohemian Grove' are found next to one another a total of ten times. 'Britney Spears' appears in 1,835 articles in the AP archive.[24]

This is not to say that the world is governed by a shadowy cabal that somehow holds the visible world of politics and business in its thrall. Organizations like the Trilateral Commission and the Bilderberg group are not omnipotent, but they are important. As Bertram Gross has pointed out: 'for imperial straight talk to mature, communication must be thoroughly protected from public scrutiny. Top elites must not only meet together frequently; they must have opportunities to work, play, and relax together for long periods of time.'[25] The debates between those who control much of the world's wealth, and who exercise enormous power as a consequence, remain for the most part unpublicized. Their power allows them to act in secret and the secrecy enhances their power. A network of institutions and more informal gatherings exists in which investors confer with politicians, opinion-formers and experts. This effectual public, one might almost say Parliament, insists on its right to privacy. Something like republican publics establish themselves behind a democratic façade. It is salutary to recall that the English Parliament in the eighteenth century long resisted efforts to publish its proceedings. The modern successors to that committee of landlords now meet, secure in the knowledge that those who would draw critical attention to their activities can be dismissed as conspiracy theorists.

Every now and again the conventions that govern elite conviviality break down and the press reveal something of the milieu shared by elected politicians, financial magnates and media owners. In October 2008 the shadow Chancellor George Osborne told journalists that New Labour's dazzling *éminence grise*, Peter Mandelson, whom he had met by chance in Corfu that summer, had 'dripped poison' into his ear about the Prime Minister, Gordon Brown. Mandelson, Osborne told the press, had been staying on the yacht of a Russian business-man called Oleg Deripaska. Osborne had met Mandelson when both were guests of a billionaire financier called Nat Rothschild. Rothschild was furious at Osborne's breach of etiquette and let it be known that Osborne too had been on the Russian's yacht, and had thought to bring along a Conservative Party fund-raiser called Andrew Feldman.[26] If Osborne had played by the rules and not made use of information gained while Rothschild's guest, we would have known nothing about the friendship between the then EU trade commissioner and a Russian magnate, or about the yacht-board antics of a senior Conservative politician. As Mandelson's spokesman at the EU pointed out, he 'draws a distinction between meetings he's had in his private time and in his public duty'.[27] And what possi-ble public interest could there be in a holiday during which two billionaires blamelessly played host to Britain's shadow Chancellor, a Conservative Party fund-raiser, and an EU trade commissioner? Oh, and another billionaire. Rupert Murdoch was also present at this avowedly private gathering.

In the United States the downfall of the lobbyist Jack Abramoff and of Congressman Randy 'Duke' Cunningham provided another glimpse of a world in which elected officials enjoy the lavish hospitality of the very rich. But in these instances, as with the earlier scandal caused by the collapse of Enron, the behaviour of at least some parties shaded into outright criminality. In the case of Enron, the full story of the criminal activity is unlikely ever to be known, in part because some of those involved are now dead. Still, what little we do know is fairly staggering.

The true extent of the links between organized crime and the political class can be acknowledged without too much fuss once they become safely historical. Joseph Kennedy's business dealings with the Chicago mob now fall into that category, as does the long working partnership between Lyndon Baines Johnson and Malcolm Wallace. In Britain, Lord Boothby's association with the Krays has come to seem almost cosy, part of a vanished world of warm beer and red telephone boxes. Many people would find the suggestion that politicians today move in the same circles as, and employ the services of, criminals outrageous or incredible, just as most people in the 1950s and '60s would have done. The very wealthy and the very powerful are for the most part able to insist on keeping their activities unpublicized. Their success in this regard leaves us with only very limited knowledge about the nature of politics broadly defined. But one only has to consider the crucial role that Enron played in the Bush campaign in 2000 to see that it would be naïve to imagine that close association between criminals and politicians is a thing of the past. Given that Enron was a criminal enterprise, Bush used the proceeds of organized crime to secure his election.[28]

The failure of the media to describe the true nature of political decision-making extends from the twilight of elite rest and recuperation to the daylight of the working week. While the media focus on the personal qualities of politicians and on a few stage-managed moments of summitry, the role of campaign donations in shaping the major parties' political agendas barely registers. Needless to say, when the connections between massive campaign contributions and the behaviour of elected governments fail to excite serious analysis in the major media, the nature and functions of important coordinating bodies remain largely unreported. For example, in Britain, the LOTIS group (the acronym stands for Liberalization of Trade in Services) rarely features in mainstream press coverage. In the last twenty-five years the *Financial Times* has mentioned its existence a total of five times. Apart from a stray mention in *The Times*, LOTIS has stayed out every other British newspaper for at least a decade.[29]

Yet, as a brief *Financial Times* article in February 2001 put it, the group is 'the established voice of the UK financial services industry for negotiations in the WTO' and consists of 'about fifteen chairman and chief executives from the UK-based financial, professional, and maritime services sector, with officials from the government, the Bank of England and the Financial Services Authority';[30] until 2006 it was headed by a former cabinet minister and European commissioner, Leon Brittan, and it continues to 'serve as the key voice of the UK financial services sector on global trade policy issues'. Its own website is more delicate than the *Financial Times* and claims merely that 'senior government representatives . . . attend as observers'.[31] As the name suggests, LOTIS seeks to remove barriers to the trade in professional services, especially financial services.

The minutes of a February 2001 meeting record the concerns of one member, Malcolm McKinnon, that they were 'vulnerable when the NGOs asked for proof of where the economic benefits of liberalisation lay'. Another member of the group, Henry Manisty of Reuters, 'wondered how business views could best be communicated to the media'. He assured his colleagues that 'his company would be most willing to give them publicity'. Another member, Neil Jaggers, raised the idea of commissioning an academic to write a research project. This research, which would cost between £50,000 and £70,000, would help them to counter the hostile NGOs and persuade developing countries to open their markets.[32]

LOTIS is at the heart of the British state's foreign policy and its work has enormous implications for the UK population as a whole. It engages in well-funded attempts to alter the climate of opinion in favour of very particular interests and does so with the encouragement and support of at least one major media institution. Yet as far as the most of the British press is concerned, LOTIS might as well not exist. Indeed, the central objectives of UK foreign policy largely escape comment in the major media. Back in 1988 the financial journalist William Keegan couldn't 'help noting that about a quarter of the UK delegation to the OECD Ministerial Meeting were press and propaganda officers of one sort or another'. He concluded that 'a lot of resources' were 'being devoted to the propagation of the British Economic Miracle'.[33]

British intelligence's rarely articulated mission to defend 'the Anglo-Saxon model of capitalism' at home runs in parallel with a concerted campaign by the Foreign Office, the various agencies of the secret state, and the City to export our version of capitalism to the rest of the world. In this the jewel in the crown is the European Union. Britain's antics in Africa and America's in Latin America are little more than a sideshow. Privatization, deregulation and liberalization, promoted by all available means, amount to an attempt to reconstruct continental Europe on lines more amenable to transnational investors. And it is this that forms the substance of the much-discussed 'special relationship'. The British state retains an imperial character, albeit as a junior partner of the United States. All this isn't a secret exactly. Those who know about it don't normally talk about it in anything other than dryly technical terms. And those who don't know mostly don't think to ask.

When Alan Greenspan admitted that the Iraq war was 'largely about oil' he said he was 'saddened' that it was 'politically inconvenient to acknowledge what everyone knows'.[34] He didn't mean 'everyone' in the ordinary sense of the word. Plenty of people didn't 'know' that the war was about oil, including the British Prime Minister. Greenspan's 'everyone' referred to the Wall Street and

City operators and the efficient, as opposed to ornate, elements in the Anglo-American state – 'everybody' meant the better-informed members of the neoliberal public. When Robert Reich wrote that at the turn of the millennium there was 'no longer any countervailing power in Washington' since business was 'in complete control of the machinery of government' he wasn't saying something that would have shocked those familiar with federal government under Bush. [35] But such claims ran contrary to what the mainstream media had been telling everyone else. The newspapers continued to find a vigorous pluralism in Washington, just as they continued wonder at the tangle of idealism, intelligence blunders and concerns over homeland security that had dragged America into Iraq.

These occasional outbreaks of elite candour have an ambiguous effect. On the one hand they might lead some people to start trying to find out for themselves what is going on. On the other hand, the blithe imperturbability of the mainstream narrative to conflicting analysis, no matter how well informed, can make the effort to pursue an independent understanding seem futile. The facts are out there, along with the lies, the distortions and the half-truths. In the absence of any means by which a better understanding might be shared, and might provide the basis for political action, there are good grounds for retreating from the bewildering contradictions of mainstream discussion. Besides, the work of establishing an alternative account will tend to distance individuals from the sites of decision, even from the shared understandings that underpin ordinary sociability. No one likes a crank, even if they happen to be right.

The forces that bear down on media institutions, and the structural features of those institutions that make them so vulnerable to this pressure, are important objects of inquiry – though largely ignored in the current media system, as one would perhaps predict. But the nature of these structural forces matters less for our immediate purposes than the demonstrable fact of systemic unreliability on the part of the major media. This unreliability perhaps more often plays out as silence than as false description: silence about the coordination between the political class and David Rothkopf's 'superclass'; silence too about the close links between state and corporate power and organized crime. The widely publicized errors discussed at the beginning of this chapter follow directly from such foundational failures.

The existence of alternative media does not materially alter the central point: that most of us don't have access to a reliable account of the world. The internet carried plenty of informed and accurate criticism of official claims before the Iraq invasion, and of mainstream economics before the collapse. But in neither case did these alternative sources of information reach an audience sufficiently large to render the prevailing fantasies inoperable.

Given the inability of the mass media to describe reality at crucial points, and the inability of the alternative media to reach a mass audience, it becomes much easier to understand the current structure of media production and consumption. Perhaps 'serious' coverage of news and current affairs struggles to find a mass audience, not because the majority are uninterested in knowing or incapable of understanding how the world works, but because 'serious' coverage is unable to explain how it does work. It provides a venue for representatives of powerful institutions and experts accredited by these same institutions to debate and compete with one another within a shared framework. It allows the elite to acknowledge and deal with the consequences of personal failings within its own ranks, and to show the wider population that it is responsive, technocratically sophisticated and morally serious. The terms of the debate and the personnel invited to take part contribute to a steady reiteration of the governing consensus. The lucrative business of celebrity does not, as Paul Dacre would like to think, draw a mass audience to the kind of 'reporting and analysis of public affairs' necessary in a healthy democracy; on the contrary, it subsidizes a deeply inadequate account of the political.

When 'serious' coverage becomes more unreliable the more important the subject under investigation is, much of the population refuses to take it seriously enough to watch it or to read it. Some of them turn instead to entertainment, celebrity and crime. This is hardly surprising, although it does provoke agonized comment from politicians and journalists who worry about the low intellectual capacities of the masses. A refusal to sit still and be told tall stories thus becomes evidence for a mass flight from maturity into the fairy-tale world of celebrity and talent shows. But the resort to trivia makes perfect sense in an environment where the sources claiming to offer reliable information do nothing of the sort.

An interest in gossip is not by any means unusual or unnatural, any more than is an interest in organized sport. It is tempting to connect the popular appetite for reality television, soap operas and talent shows to a collapse in sociability. On this model, atomized individuals construct an emotional world from the products of popular culture. Though social isolation is a problem and the consumption of medi-ated sociability is growing ever more avid, the connections between them are not at all straightforward. The temptation to believe that the one simply causes the other reflects perhaps a certain fear of pleas-ure, and particularly popular pleasure, in the critical imagination.

Celebrity provides the raw material for a super-refined form of gossip. Our propensity to trade embarrassing or salacious details about other people can go to work on child-stars in meltdown, the primal fascination of beautiful people having sex with one another, or the jolt of the sudden death of the far-off familiar. When compared with the daily bread of gossip about co-workers and people you know, celebrity coverage is a kind of cake. But the popular appetite for celebrity gossip doesn't in itself tell us a huge amount about the wider population's capacity for self-government. Given that alleg-edly serious coverage repeatedly turns out to be fantastical, it is hardly surprising that other elements of the media ecology have ballooned out to take its place. And while it is easy to recognize the distortions of some forms of story-telling, the absence of accurate descriptions of key aspects of our shared life rearranges the landscape of representation as a whole in ways that are much more difficult to appreciate. Literature and drama suffer when purportedly factual descriptions degenerate into simple-minded morality tales.

The description of the general culture presented by the mass media takes on an ever more hallucinatory quality. The population is denounced for its lack of interest in descriptions of the world produced by the serious media, even though these descriptions repeatedly turn out to be based on absurd fantasies. Allegedly serious commentators and critics worry about the mental incompetence of the masses, while they themselves mouth one *non sequitur* after another. In such circumstances, a genuine public opinion, in the sense of a rationally grounded and widely shared account of the world, is unable to form. And as we shall see, the media's failure to describe the world of power combines with a settled inability to describe us to our fellow citizens.

CHAPTER EIGHT

Estranged From Each Other

I N THE UNITED States consistent majorities favour policies that the two main parties and most experts and commentators either ignore or reject. In foreign policy this gap is especially pronounced. In *The Foreign Policy Disconnect*, Benjamin Page and Marshall Bouton explore popular preferences and American policy in considerable detail and conclude persuasively that 'the actual foreign policies of the United States have often differed markedly from the policies that most Americans want'.[1] For example, the authors show that the US population is much keener to strengthen the UN and much more likely to believe that the protection of jobs should be a very important foreign policy goal than are the policy-makers. As Page has written elsewhere, the evidence suggests that 'the influence of the public was barely discernible' on foreign policy. By contrast, he adds, business leaders and foreign policy experts have had a 'big effect' on decision-makers in government.[2]

In domestic politics strong support for state-funded healthcare has been recorded in opinion polls in the United States for more than 40 years. Yet when mainstream journalists notice this support, they can dismiss it with astonishing insouciance. As Noam Chomsky has noted, during the 2004 election the *New York Times* explained that Kerry had stressed that 'his plan for expanding access to health insurance would not create a new government program'. The paper explained that this was because there was 'so little political support for government intervention in the health care market in the United States'.[3] Political support, according to the *New York Times*, was not something that the population could give on an issue as consequential as healthcare. The newspaper had the tact not to mention whose preferences translated into political support.

President Obama introduced a measure of healthcare reform in the spring of 2010. But while it expands healthcare coverage, the legislation leaves the private health-insurance industry substantially intact and falls far short of what most Americans say that they want. In January 2009 a *New York Times*/CBS poll found that 59 per cent of Americans wanted to see a 'single-payer' system introduced, in which the state guaranteed universal provision. Nine months later, after a furious propaganda campaign by the private healthcare lobby, 65 per cent of those polled by the *New York Times* still supported a 'public option', in which the state would offer healthcare insurance to all citizens in competition with existing private insurers.[4] Much to the satisfaction of the major healthcare providers no such public option features in the much-praised reforms.

At times, the ability of the media in America to ignore, dismiss or misunderstand the public's preferences has achieved an astonishing, if presumably unconscious, virtuosity. In a study of the way opinion-poll results are interpreted, for example, Justin Lewis was struck by 'the degree to which a whole range of apparently popular opinions can be ignored if they fall outside the general political framework advanced by political elites'. According to Lewis, public opinion that appears 'centrist or conservative' will be given more publicity than opinion that appears to favour, say, universal healthcare or limits on the power of big business.[5]

The media also gives extensive publicity to popular opinion when it seems quirky or eccentric. In September 1996 a Gallup poll found that 71 per cent of Americans believed that their government knew more about UFOs than it was willing to reveal.[6] This lack of faith in government institutions received quite extensive exposure in the print media. More than 20 newspapers mentioned the poll's findings, including the *Miami Herald*, the *Denver Post*, the *Cleveland Plain Dealer* and, predictably enough, the *New York Times*.[7] In the same year a Harris poll reported that 71 per cent of Americans thought that business had too much power over too many aspects of life. A database search could only find two mentions of this poll, in the *Seattle Times* and *USA Today*.[8]

While the newspapers tended to treat the Gallup poll finding as evidence of popular irrationality – headlines like 'Come On Down' and 'Aliens Invade Americans' Minds!' were characteristic of the way the story was presented – the 71 per cent of the population who thought the US government knew more about UFOs than it was telling them were technically correct. Many reports of unidentified flying objects would have been classified at the time the poll was taken. Well-founded doubts about the extent of government candour mutated in the journalistic imagination into evidence that almost everyone they didn't know harboured fantasies about an imminent alien invasion.

When events compel the mainstream media to take notice of the population's attitude towards the country's dominant interests it takes considerable pains to frame discussion in ways that minimize the significance of what is being reported. Again in 1996, Richard Harwood set out in the *Washington Post* to 'make sense' of the presidential campaign. To do so he shifted from the political to the psychological:

> We are riven in both parties with fears and suspicions. The common ground includes fear about the power of big corporations (82 percent of Democrats, 62 percent of Republicans). They have common fears about 'dangerous books', 46 percent of Democrats and 48 percent of Republicans want to ban them from school libraries. . .[9]

According to Harwood just about everything troubling the American people should be understood as part of a cross-party culture of 'fears and suspicions'. Harwood's approach helps him avoid the obvious question – whether some of these fears and suspicions might in some sense be justified. This framework for explanation encourages his readers to marvel at a general and mysterious national neurosis, rather than to consider whether corporations, being distrusted by large and stable majorities of the population, ought to be treated with a little more suspicion by the media on which the population relies for information about the world beyond its direct experience.

A little less than a decade later, in 2005, in the wake of accounting scandals at Enron, Tyco and elsewhere, another Harris poll reported that a full 90 per cent of Americans thought business had too much influence in the political process. This time the *New York Times* found space to report the poll. But it did so in an article that carried the headline 'New Surveys Show That Big Business Has a P.R. Problem'.[10] The vast majority of people in the United States thought that large companies were a threat to democracy. But the *New York Times* decided that the problem was not to do with the way business influences the political process, rather, it lay in the way business communicates with the population. Again the writer avoids the obvious question – whether 90 per cent of the population might have a point. The population's fears and suspicions must be caused by faulty communications; their possible basis in fact escapes consideration.

Despite the evidence that popular preferences only selectively achieve publicity, commentators in America often worry about the political system's excessive populism, its susceptibility to 'democratic distemper'. President Clinton was singled out for his demagogic pandering and mocked for his reliance on polls. But far from bending to the popular will as expressed in the opinion polls and focus groups he so assiduously studied, in 1994 Clinton presided

over what Page and Bouton have called 'the sharpest observed diver-
gence between policy-makers and the public on economic foreign
policy issues' when he invested a huge amount of effort in securing
the North American Free Trade Area.[11] Clinton deferred to the polls
when deciding what kind of holiday he should take. He used them to
shape his message and to help craft micro-policies that would appeal
to electorally important demographics. But when it came to major
decisions regarding America's management of the global economy,
popular preferences were something to be finessed where possible
and ignored when necessary.

Many descriptions of the population as a whole reprise the themes
and emotional resources of both sexist and racist polemic. It has long
been considered sophisticated to inveigh against the idiocy and igno-
rance of the masses. It was Virginia Woolf, after all, who imagined
'that anonymous monster, the man in the street' as 'a vast, almost
featureless, almost shapeless jelly of human stuff . . . occasionally wobbling this way or that as some instinct of hate, revenge, or
admiration bubbles up beneath it'.[12] Recycling the fatuities of 1930s
Bloomsbury remains a short cut to intellectual respectability. In
contrast, the conclusion of the American scholars David Sears and
Carolyn Funk – that 'the general public thinks about most political
issues, most of the time, in a disinterested frame of mind'[13] – makes
little or no impact on a prejudice that serves so many pressing needs.
An indifference to evidence of disinterest and discrimination in
the general population signals one's seriousness and sophistication,
one's acquired immunity to the contagion of mere fact. As a result,
the inarticulate majority becomes the last acceptable recipient of
unfounded contempt.

In Britain, reporting also tends to marginalize serious objections
to the established order among the general population. In 2006 the
Joseph Rowntree Charitable Trust and the Joseph Rowntree Reform
Trust published a wide-ranging review of Britain's political economy.
After a long and exhaustive consultation process the report noted

that the 'research and evidence displays that many people feel business has too great an influence over government at the expense of the "ordinary" citizen'.[14] This finding, which echoes American attitudes towards the political power of business, did not find its way into the report's executive summary, except in an isolated and unexplained recommendation that 'ministerial meetings with representatives of business including lobbyists should be logged and listed on a monthly basis'.[15] In media coverage of the report, which included extensive write-ups in the *Independent* and the *Guardian* and summaries of its findings in the *Daily Telegraph*, the *Sunday Telegraph*, the *Observer*, *The Times*, the *Sunday Times* and the *Financial Times*, the view that business had excessive political power did not feature. The matter of donations to the political parties was mentioned, as were a number of the commission's recommendations for constitutional reform. But a key element in any serious attempt to account for the growing distance between the population at large and the ruling establishment was missing from the mainstream coverage.

In Britain too, it is usually taken as a given that the political class are cowed by, and deferential to, the demands of the population. Steve Richards articulates this consensus when he claims that 'politicians are so wary of moving away from majority opinion that they follow focus groups obsessively'.[16] Tony Blair, like Clinton, was berated for his shallow populism, but New Labour's intense interest in popular attitudes did not stop it from pursuing policies that most people strongly opposed. Blair, as noted above, sought to appear 'to empathise with public concern and then channel it into the correct course' – the latter being something that he was supposedly best placed to discern. Focus groups and opinion-poll data did not stop his government from seeking to privatize the National Health Service, though they doubtless encouraged ministers to couch their policies in terms of the more positive-sounding notion of 'reform'.

Again, as in the United States, when British intellectuals do notice the popular distrust of big business and other powerful institutions they are every bit as likely as their American counterparts to account for it in ways that foreclose any discussion of these institutions' behaviour and the extent to which that behaviour might be the cause of the distrust. In the Reith Lectures of 2000, for example, the philosopher Onora O'Neill argued that what others saw as evidence of a 'crisis of trust' in British culture really pointed to a 'culture of suspicion'. While people said that they didn't trust big companies, they continued to use their products. While they said that they didn't trust journalists, they continued to buy newspapers; 'the evidence suggests that we still constantly place trust in many of the institutions and professions we profess not to trust'.[17] O'Neill's reasoning is as feeble as it is welcome to the harassed managers of those institutions beset by popular scepticism.

Readers can trust a newspaper's racing tips while not believing a word of its political coverage. A patient can swallow a drug without swallowing the idea that privately owned corporations can be trusted to shape medical science in the general interest. A customer can trust a supermarket chain not to poison him without trusting the same chain to respect the interests of the communities in which it seeks to build new stores. That we continue to engage with institutions that we profess not to trust does not remotely prove that we trust them really and are only mouthing the conventional wisdom of a 'culture of suspicion'.

O'Neill doesn't think appear to think that powerful institutions are untrustworthy. Accordingly, she shows no interest in the actions of big business or government. She makes no mention of high-level lobbying, of the various attempts to manipulate the climate of opinion, the habitual tax avoidance of large companies and their reliance on cheap labour in the developing world. In retailing the mysteries of a 'culture of suspicion', O'Neill finds the perfect means to dodge the issues: Perhaps we say we don't trust business and government because it is the fashionable thing to say? Or perhaps our stated concerns are a surrogate for some other anxiety? Perhaps it has something to do with the angst created by sensational or superficial reporting, or by the pursuit of perfect accountability, or by modernity itself? A vague cultural trend thus becomes the focus of O'Neill's concern, and this, rather than the recorded conduct of powerful institutions, is then supposed to account for the widespread lack of faith in society's governing institutions.

Members of the British administrative elite like to reprise the themes raised in Onora O'Neill's lectures. In a speech in January 2008, Mark Thompson, the Director General of the BBC, recognized that there was 'a deep and growing scepticism about whether the system or the individuals involved in it can ever be trusted to reveal what's really going on'.[18] Given that the BBC had failed to reveal what was really going on in Britain's financial sector until the summer of the previous year, Thompson might have wanted to concede that the sceptics had a point. Instead he took it for granted that the widely reported and growing suspicion of government and other powerful institutions was exaggerated. A significant proportion of the population had, he said, 'a distorted view of reality', and it was this that needed to change, not reality, if trust was to be restored. After all, as he couldn't resist pointing out, 30 per cent of the British population believed that the government was covering up evidence of extra-terrestrial life. Not only that, Thompson claimed that 'the less you trust politicians and public institutions, the more likely you are to believe in outré conspiracy theories, not to mention witches and warlocks'.[19]

According to Thompson the population are not sceptical of politicians because the latter are not telling them what is going on, but because communication between the elite and the population has somehow malfunctioned. People don't understand the complex language of modern political administration and, for reasons Thompson did not explain, think that 'the system [drives] politicians and others to distort the truth'. There is, he argued, a gulf between a technocratic elite and the wider population, and the BBC has an important role to play in bridging that gap, with more coverage of Parliament and more thoughtful and reflective presentation of policies. The notion that these technocratic and essentially trustworthy 'people in public life' should be joined in effective decision-making by the bulk of the population did not seem to occur to him. Policy-making, like the communications business, is the preserve of experts.

The problem to address, according to Thompson, is popular fear and incomprehension when faced with the technocratic complexity of modern administration. The BBC, he argued, had to do a better job explaining what was going on. As the authors of *The New Effective Public Manager* had warned in 1995, 'when you deal with the general public you should expect its members to have a limited understanding of the complexity of most issues'.[20] It is a good idea to find that the general population doesn't understand the issues properly, since that way you can characterize the criticisms that come your way as evidence of a failure to engage in the complexities of contemporary life, or as what Thompson called 'outré conspiracy theories'. Thompson and other senior administrators in the media only have to engage with the population when it concurs with their world-view. The regular failures of the media to state the blindingly obvious do nothing to shake Thompson's conviction that scepticism is based on a distorted view of reality, rather than on a reasoned assessment of the media's performance. Far from having the means to talk back to the media, as in Wright Mills's ideal type of the public, we are only audible once we echo their governing assumptions about the nature of the political realm.

A related strand in British elite thought centres on the notion that the media has become too hostile to politicians and thereby undermined faith in government. According to these critics, the media have obsessively sought to find evidence of hypocrisy or mendacity in ways that are both damaging to democracy and savagely unfair to individual politicians. In a speech at the end of his time as Prime Minister Tony Blair argued that in an intensely competitive journalistic culture 'the fear of missing out means today's media, more than ever before, hunts in a pack. In these modes it is like a feral beast, just tearing people and reputations to bits.'[21] Certainly much political coverage is cynical and sarcastic, and those charged with describing the political world often seem to hold professional politicians in contempt. Journalists justify their conduct on the grounds that the politicians are trying to manipulate the reporting process and so both suspicion and tough questioning are justified. The expenses scandal suggests that there is something to this.

But while journalists are merciless to politicians as private individuals, they rarely challenge the right of the major political parties to determine the limits of widely publicized debate and discussion. They do not, and cannot, call into question the fundamental assumptions of those who control the institutions they report. When an issue looms larger than the foibles of individual politicians and the manoeuvrings for partisan advantage within agreed zones of controversy – in other words when the political classes present a united front, as with basic matters of economic management and the mysteries of war – political journalists for the most part do no more than relay what those in power are doing or thinking.[22] To do otherwise would doubtless seem like falling for outré conspiracy theories, even when conspiracies are taking place. Scrutiny of the political process is combative and abrasive at the level of individual competence and character, and it attends closely to disagreements within the elite. But it co-exists with a quite placid acceptance of the governing consensus. And this is to be expected if we bear in mind Pierre Bourdieu's comment that journalism 'is a very powerful profession made up of very fragile individuals'.[23] Journalists find it very difficult to build a career, and therefore secure publicity for their work, if they refuse to accept the basic assumptions of those they report and on whom they rely for newsworthy information.

Those who are comfortable with our current arrangements sometimes argue that the preferences of the governed and their elected representatives don't *really* diverge in the ways outlined. People might say that they want policies that are resisted by the parties they vote for. But if they continue to vote for politicians who repeatedly frustrate them, they must be broadly happy with the results they get. Candidates for office, to the extent that they ignore what the population says about key issues, are only recognizing that what people do at election time matters more than what they tell pollsters. And as for those who don't vote, they too must be more or less happy with things as they are, or they would organize to change them through the political process. Their silence implies consent, or at least an apathy that might be regrettable, but for which the existing institutions cannot be blamed.

Yet the mere fact of voting hardly demonstrates unqualified support for prevailing conditions. We can continue to engage in the political process even if we are deeply sceptical about it in important respects. Voting for a given party doesn't mean that we think they are anything other than the least putrid apple in a very rotten barrel. There is even less reason to think that those who abstain do so out of settled contentment with the status quo. Nevertheless, journalists feel justified in limiting debate for the most part to those matters upon which the major political parties disagree, regardless of the facts they collectively choose to ignore.

Individuals cannot be manipulated at will by a deceitful and sophisticated media class; we are not necessarily caught in a state of false consciousness in any simple sense. The evidence suggests that many people are capable of developing stable and reasoned political positions on the basis of their experiences, and through a critical reading of the information available to them. Their policy preferences can remain consistently at odds with those of political and economic decision-makers in spite of a media environment that rarely notices these preferences. If they don't pay close attention to the goings-on in Westminster and Washington, for all that this excites liberal angst about dumbing down, their decision to concentrate on sport or celebrity might well derive from a reasoned assessment of their chances of securing the policies they want. On the other hand, popular culture clearly isn't a seething mass of subversive counter-readings, a constant decoding of dominant narratives. The biases, evasions and omissions of the mainstream media undermine our capacity for self-government in important ways. Nevertheless, on a number of key issues people know what they think and are remarkably resistant to attempts to change their minds.

The long success of the Labour–Conservative and Democratic–Republican duopolies only provides evidence of informed consent for the current political and economic structures if we have a clear sense of what our fellow citizens believe and would like to see done by their government. If we believe that an electorally insignificant minority shares our views on particular issues we will have no incentive to organize to pursue policies based on those views. We will conclude, reluctantly but rationally, that we are at the margins of opinion and, so long as we are kept innocent of the state of popular opinion, we will reach this conclusion even if – unbeknownst to us – most of our fellow citizens share our preferences. The incessant noise in the media about the urgent necessity to 'promote free trade' or about the dangers of socialized medicine might matter less than the almost uncanny silence that greets awkward information about popular preferences and beliefs.

The media system cannot, as its mainstream critics sometimes demand of it, 'restore faith' in the governing institutions and those who run them. The same 2005 poll that prompted the *New York Times* to worry about big business's public relations problem found that only 4 per cent of those polled thought that the media were very trustworthy. And despite a barrage of propaganda about heroic business leaders, only 2 per cent thought that Fortune 500 CEOs were very trustworthy. While it is always good fun to review the failings of the major media and the villainies of business, they are not news to most of the population. What most of us do not appreciate is the extent to which others share our scepticism.

But the media have a much easier time persuading us that most of our fellow citizens are either tolerably content with the way things are, or else are preoccupied with learning the truth about UFOs. The population's actual views are rarely considered worth reporting, unless they confirm elite prejudices about the craziness of the masses, or else provide evidence of properly directed engagement in matters that the elite wish to see discussed. A population takes an important step to becoming a public when it is able to represent its own views to itself with some tolerable degree of accuracy. At the present time neither the American nor the British people have much of an idea what their fellow citizens think about the issues that their elected representatives and their media discuss at such length. They have even less of an idea what their fellow citizens think about issues that those who set the terms of acceptable debate decline to discuss. And even if as individuals we are able to challenge and reject claims in the media on the basis of personal experience, alternative sources of information and independent judgements of plausibility, we have few grounds for thinking that our views are widely shared. This then is the second element in the current crisis: we have become a mystery to each other.

In modern industrial society citizens cannot come to know one another's political views through the spontaneous activities of daily life. The unofficial publics of civil society no longer meet with the same regularity; we have perhaps become less sociable over the last generation and this may have exacerbated the problem. But as citizens of large nations we must ultimately depend on mediated information to form a picture of the wider world, including a picture of our fellow citizens and the world they wish to see. We depend on the media to tell us how much we resemble one another but they tell us that the people we don't know are slavering Evangelical fascists, recovering alien abductees, or well-adjusted supporters of one of the two main political parties. What they tell us leaves us feeling isolated, even desperate. But we can always go shopping. There at least, in the reassuringly bright light of the well-stocked supermarket, we can express ourselves, in close proximity to others, with whom we rarely speak.

CHAPTER NINE

Estranged From Ourselves

The end of the common world has come when it is only seen under one aspect and is permitted to present itself in only one perspective.

Hannah Arendt

F ROM THE MID-1970s the competitive individual seeking satisfaction through market exchange became increasingly influential
as a model for human self-understanding. Political leaders in both
Britain and the United States insisted that there was no alternative
to a system organized around self-interest and the rest of the culture
largely fell into line. Humans have a habit of describing themselves
and then acting in ways that conform to the description. One study
by the economist Robert Frank gives some hint of the way that free
market ideology changed the world it purported only to describe.
Frank found that first-year economics students became less cooperative and honest over the course of their studies. When Frank
compared the fledgling economists with astronomers he found that
the star-gazers became more trustworthy and cooperative in the
same period.[1]

Kant remarks in the conclusion of his *Critique of Practical Reason*
that 'two things fill the mind with ever new and increasing admiration and awe, the oftener and the more steadily we reflect on them:
the starry heavens above and the moral law within'.[2] He would have
been pleased to know that the contemplation of the heavens does
nothing to make us less attentive to the moral law within. The claims

and assumptions of neoliberal economics have had somewhat greater publicity in the last generation than either astronomy or the moral law, with effects that, though not strictly measurable, can nevertheless be surmised.

The neoliberal description of society, in which self-seeking individuals compete under the watchful eye of an enabling state, is radically at odds with reality. The economy is not an entrepreneurial free-for-all but a space dominated by very large organizations, where the state uses taxpayers' money to subsidize favoured sectors. For the most part, the individual competes with other individuals for employment and promotion. Bureaucratic politics in steep hierarchical systems, rather than the mechanics of market competition, determine the division of rewards. As early as the 1930s it was obvious that '[g]roup activity . . . the extreme division of labor in large scale enterprise necessarily imply not individualism but cooperation and the acceptance of authority almost to the point of autocracy'.[3] In such circumstances, as Wendell Berry noted, 'one does not think to improve oneself by becoming better at what one is doing or by assuming some measure of public responsibility in order to improve local conditions; one thinks to improve oneself . . . by "moving up" to a "place of higher consideration"'.[4]

Nevertheless, fanciful though it was, the neoliberal account of politics and economics purported to offer an account of both human nature and the good life. Happiness was to be found in the marketplace, not in the business of political debate and participation. In an environment characterized by competition between individuals there was little time for citizenship in the straitened form offered by pluralism, much less for the heroic public action of classical republicanism. Indeed, longer working hours and longer commutes made it ever more difficult for those who wanted to remain competitive to enjoy even the ordinary endeavours and satisfactions of private life outside the workplace.

Neoliberalism wasn't the only resource available to those who wanted to foster competitive individualism. A reinvigorated social Darwinism purported to tell us huge amounts about human nature; as the product of evolution, the human mind itself bore the imprints of millions of years of competitive pressure. Darwinist psychologists were not shy about making biology the basis for political claims. Edward Wilson, one of the most influential writers in the field, once declared of Marxism: 'wonderful theory, wrong species'.[5] Even when they didn't draw simple inferences from biology to politics, evolutionary psychologists had an unnerving confidence when they pronounced on human nature. Steven Pinker is fond of telling interviewers that a 1969 strike by the police in Montreal shook him out of his naïve anarchism: 'within hours mayhem and rioting broke out and the Mounties had to be called in to restore order. It instilled in me that one's convictions can be subjected to empirical test.'[6]

Pinker appears to think that the 'empirical test' of the strike established that human beings are nasty and brutish and that only a powerful state can stave off a war of all against all. Hobbes's vision of man as an animal that must be restrained by superior force thus finds confirmation from a renowned popularizer of evolutionary theory. But Pinker succumbs to the same fallacy as Hobbes and bases his convictions about humanity's nature, and hence its political potential, on the behaviour of individuals enmeshed in the particular circumstances of a particular form of life. In the seventeenth century it was called the fallacy of the court. Renovated in the late twentieth century it vested evolutionary theory with an unfortunate cultural power and allowed Pinker and others to dignify their own assumptions about the limits of political action as the discoveries of an indifferent science.[7] But much like Hobbes and Locke, the psychological Darwinists all too often drew on an account of man in a state of nature that simply asserted what it claimed to prove.

Popular culture and mainstream commentary bound neoliberalism and psychological Darwinism together to tell a story about human nature in which the only possible routes to a better life were to found through personal exertion in the market. Neoliberalism was the prose version of this, the dominant ideology of our times. It claimed straightforwardly that individuals are rationally selfish and that they are best understood to be motivated not by considerations of justice, compassion or the common good, but by the drive to better their own condition. Markets, by providing a medium of free exchange, allowed these selfish creatures the means to pursue their desires without recourse to violence. The notion of man as the culmination of millions of years of competition provided a kind of complementary poetry of human nature, that was all but irresistible in its awful psychological effects, but that did not always need to resolve itself into plain speech.

In 1976 Richard Dawkins presented a popular version of the gene-centred account of evolution, *The Selfish Gene*, which went on to become a massive bestseller. But while Dawkins wanted to insist that talking about a gene 'as if it were consciously working out how best to increase its success' is a harmless 'language of convenience . . . unless it happens to fall into the hands of those ill-equipped to understand it',[8] the notion that the basic units of life were selfish was something that few of us were well equipped to treat in purely figurative terms, especially as Anglo-American society became markedly more competitive. And Dawkins didn't help matters when he went on to describe human beings as robots constructed to do the bidding of their genes. This was a language all too convenient for the culture of neoliberalism, since the selfish gene seemed to explain so much in terms agreeable to those who had done well in a competitive society. So what if success required that one cut a few corners, tell a few lies, or connive in a few crimes? We are, after all, robots constructed by our genes; what else can we do but their bidding? One can see how misunderstanding might have crept in. Darwinism seemed to confirm the logic of market competition. It comforted those who had succeeded in the neoliberal frenzy and confronted those who could not or would not compete with a defeat that was not political but natural, a consequence of genetic unfitness.

If economics makes students less trustworthy and more self-seeking, then the account of human nature offered by evolutionary psychology could hardly fail to make us more wary of our generous impulses and less likely to set moral limits on our efforts to secure our own interests in an intensifying struggle for existence. The reasoning that connected selfishness and selfish genes was mistaken, but it made good sense to be mistaken when everyone else seemed to be making the same mistake. We are all too ready to conform to the stories we hear about our nature and it would be reckless to imagine that the new Darwinism has less prescriptive power, for all that its proponents might want to insist on its celestial distance from day-to-day ordinary moral reasoning.

Perhaps the twin triumph of psychological Darwinism and neoliberalism would have mattered less if individuals and societies had flourished in the 30 years since 1980. In fact the long experiment in neoliberal economics with Darwinian characteristics has in many respects been a human welfare disaster. The clinical psychologist Bruce Levine notes that

> an estimated 20 to 25 percent of Americans use psychiatric drugs; 10 to 15 percent abuse alcohol and illegal psychotropic drugs; and 7 to 12 percent compulsively gamble. Millions more compulsively view television, video games and pornography; play the stock market; overeat; shop for things they don't need; and flee their helplessness and hopelessness in countless other ways.[9]

In Britain the situation is every bit as desperate. The Department of Health's Alcohol Needs Assessment Project estimated in 2004 that 26 per cent of British adults – around 8.2 million people – have what they call an 'alcohol use disorder'.[10] The most recent NHS report on drug misuse claimed that 10.1 per cent of adults in England had used one or more illicit drug in the previous year.[11] According to the UK government, by 2000 one adult in six was suffering from a neurotic disorder, for the most part anxiety, depression, or both.[12] In their book *The Spirit Level*, Richard Wilkinson and Kate Pickett detail how almost all forms of social distress have increased significantly in the period of the neoliberal ascendancy. For example, when large-scale studies of males born in 1958 and in 1970 were compared, the levels of depression in early adulthood were found to be twice as high in the younger group.[13] Rates of incarceration, obesity and teenage pregnancy have all increased in Britain and the United States in the same period. The authors plausibly argue that rising income inequality is central to understanding this rising tide of dysfunction and unhappiness.

Inequality increases social distance and so promotes distress.[14] People withdraw from the common experience of life into increasingly isolated enclaves. As different groups cease to meet on terms of reasonable equality they lose a sense of shared moral responsibility. The majority begin to feel humiliated by the sense of being excluded from the pleasures and satisfactions that high status seems to deliver. The picture is complicated in Anglo-America where so many fortunes are made through criminal, quasi-criminal and anti-social activity in the financial markets. Yet many experience their reluctance to join this free-for-all as a kind of shame. The collapse of solidarity breeds further criminality, class antagonism and a culture of mutual distrust as the rich come to inhabit a different world and the connection between virtue and status becomes ever more attenuated.

As Anna Minton points out, we have known for a long time that the individual's opportunity to flourish depends on social factors. During the Second World War the British population became less mentally distressed, contrary to the predictions of many psychiatrists.[15] The sense of shared jeopardy and the introduction of universal services both served to reduce levels of what the social scientist Richard Titmus called 'social disparagement'. The war brought a sense of common purpose and sharply reduced the levels of economic inequality. People felt dignified and elevated during the six years in which they worked together to save their country and their way of life; the war qualified hierarchies by asserting a civic equality. Overwhelmingly committed to the immediate task of national survival and to the creation of a new society after the war, the British became happier as they came to resemble an autonomous public.

So, reducing equality and establishing a sense of shared citizenship through participation in civic life would presumably lead to lower levels of personal distress. Yet the most common responses to individual misery and social dysfunction – from pharmaceutical drugs and strategies to address alleged deficiencies in childrearing to 'zero tolerance' policing and a return to traditional values – avoid discussing why social problems have been increasing in recent years in some countries but not in others. At best these supposed remedies will be only accidentally and intermittently effective; at worst they will distract us from serious thought about the kind of society we want and from policies that may prove more effective in addressing the competitive individualism in conditions of general cynicism that has become the cultural default.

As the rich grew richer they were able to spend some of their new wealth on promoting ideas that blunted opposition to their plans and that made them feel good. Those lucky few who captured so much more of the national income in Britain and the United States understandably liked the system that had served them so well. They thought they deserved their good fortune and wanted everyone else to think so too. The defensive and sometimes panicky response of investors when previously passive groups began to assert themselves in the 1960s and 1970s developed into a campaign to reassert ideas last taken seriously in the years before the Wall Street Crash. Those who secured vast fortunes in the period after 1980 wanted to hear that what they had done was both rational and natural. Economics and popular science responded to the demand.

By degrees, the conviction that humans are narrowly self-seeking began to seep into popular as well as elite culture. The kind of retail Machiavellianism found in books like *The 48 Laws of Power* contributed to a pervasive paranoia about the motivations of others.[16] This paranoia in turn undermined efforts to engage in collective efforts to understand and to change society. Solutions could only be sought at the level of the individual, supposedly because humans are selfish and as such cooperation in pursuit of shared interests is somehow impossible. What Virginia Woolf called 'that anonymous monster the Man in the street' was a product of millions of years of evolution whose every move could be predicted by the calculus of narrow self-interest.

The culture industry broadly defined continues to leave unchallenged an account of human nature that is at odds with the observable facts; business books treat management as a branch of primatology or of military strategy while popular science repeatedly discovered how competition had made us self-interested. In such circumstances personal advancement appears to be the only way to escape the sadness or distress that current conditions engender. Not surprisingly, in an environment where economic crises are explained away as natural phenomena and the dominant strands in social science insist on our fundamental selfishness, we have found ourselves increasingly unable to think in terms of collective rather than individual responses to problems that face us all.

As skilled jobs are replaced by software or move offshore, white-collar workers are encouraged to make themselves employable again by becoming ever more upbeat and cooperative. They have lost their jobs because their thought processes are somehow at fault; returning to stable employment is a matter of fixing some glitch in their internal programming. As competition for reasonably well-paid jobs intensifies, the newly unemployed try to become the sort of person that another employer will want. If it is the individual, not the economic system, that is at fault then it is the individual, not the economic system, that must be reformed. This emphasis on personal responsibility and agency becomes decidedly sinister when we recall Larry Summers' remarks about the higher levels of structural unemployment that we can now expect. No matter how hard we try, the current economic system needs fewer and fewer of us.

Those made depressed or anxious by uncertainty in the workplace are offered treatments that barely register, much less challenge, the structural forces that generate such psychological pressure and material disruption. These individually tailored responses to distress vary in sophistication from the bromides of the positive-thinking tradition to more sophisticated regimes that help reduce the debilitating effects of ingrained patterns of thought or of the impact of upbringing on adult self-understanding. They also include drugs that are supposed to correct chemical imbalances in the brain, advice on changes to our diet and our lifestyle, exercise regimes, and so on.

The Secret, and an endless succession of books, websites and DVDs like it, offers variations on a formula that is now more than century old and has its origins in the culture of consumption that developed in the United States in the latter part of the nineteenth century.[17] The broad outlines of this formula were stated, appropriately enough, by *Success* magazine in 1903: 'If you want to get the most out of life, just make up your mind that you were made to be happy, that you are a happiness-machine, as well as a work-machine . . . Think positive, creative, happy thoughts and your harvest of good things will be abundant.'[18] This hopeful message has echoed down the decades. The mechanism that connects your wishes to the world varies according to circumstances. Sometimes esoteric Eastern wisdom supplies the link, sometimes it comes from the power of prayer. Recently quantum entanglement, what Einstein called 'spooky action at a distance', has provided a scientific gloss for the central claim of self-help, that the world can be made to give us what we want if we only reform our state of mind.

Like neoliberalism and certain readings of evolutionary psychology, positive thinking takes the solitary individual as its point of departure. Like them it offers us the chance to accommodate ourselves to a higher reality, to change through self-scrutiny and individual effort so that we are no longer in conflict with how things have to be. But the structure of society, the nature of the institutions and ideas with which we co-exist, the forms of collective life to which we have access, all play a part in determining whether we are tolerably happy or succumb to mental illness. We currently leave people to choose one or other individualistic way out of anxiety and depression. But we have largely ignored the role that specifically political action can play in improving individual well-being. This is not to say that we are simply the victims of a hostile environment. We are perfectly capable of making our lives a misery through the ordinary tragedies of love and ambition. But positive thinking and pharmaceutical drugs predominate in our sense of how we might cope with distress, perhaps because they hold out the hope that we can achieve happiness without addressing the structure of society.

Competitive individualism and income inequality are very bad for us, yet they feature much less prominently in discussions of unhappiness than serotonin deficiency. Political participation, extensive social ties and, above all, broadly equal incomes correlate closely with individual happiness. Every now and then someone will suggest that a public response to private distress might be appropriate, but they will take their place among a multitude of entrepreneurs offering happiness now, in just a few simple steps. Marketers who are comfortable operating within the culture's account of what it is to be happy and fulfilled corroborate, and are corroborated by, the vast ingenuity of commercial persuasion. By comparison, collective responses to the epidemic of distress in Britain and the United States that hold out some hope of being effective seem unrealistic, beside the point, or downright dangerous.

The self-help industry offers endlessly compelling and reliably temporary solutions to individual unhappiness. We are on our own, we are told, and we must take care of ourselves. It seems reasonable to conclude that our happiness is in our own hands, a private possession that we can acquire if we adopt the right mental routines, whether they derive from New Thought, Eastern mysticism, or quantum mechanics. An alternative perspective, one that takes into account the social and institutional circumstances of life and seeks to reform their pernicious effects on the self, seems somehow confused. How can I help myself if I don't concentrate all my energies on myself? And so the striving for happiness turns inwards, away from the machinery of effectual change towards an ever more extensive regime of self-administered mind control. Self-help thinking suggests that we respond to the absence of a public status by focusing even more intently on our own states of mind. We are encouraged to think that our private selves can be helped through strategies that are themselves limited to the private sphere. In this insistence that our problems belong to us – that they are, like our happiness, a kind of property – the governing ideology achieves its individuating triumph. In our isolation we re-enact the same doomed effort to achieve stable possession of what can never belong to us as individuals.

It is easy to see, and see through, some of the more desperate excesses of this individualist response to the pressures of modernity – to see how *The Secret* torments its millions of readers with the promise that everything in their reach, if only they will believe hard enough, or how certain sorts of business books tantalize the normally human with dreams of sociopathic clarity. But a general confusion affects the entire field of speech about the self. Literary culture becomes part of a general crisis alongside the barely literate productions of the self-help industry. Shirley Brice Heath, commenting on her studies of readers of 'substantive works of fiction', has argued that literature provides a refuge from the insistent idiocies of the wider culture. Nearly all readers said that literary novels were 'the only places where there was some civic, public hope of coming to grips with the ethical, philosophical and socio-political dimensions of life that were elsewhere treated so simplistically'. In contrast with such treatments, Heath highlights the principled refusal of serious fiction to reduce the dilemmas of life – the conflicts of loyalty and unruliness of desire – to black and white issues. Serious novels do not paint things 'as good guys versus bad guys', they are 'everything that pop psychology is not'. Serious novels provide readers with resources that help them to handle 'their inability to have a totally predictable life'.[19]

But novels are not quite everything that pop psychology is not; serious works of fiction remain an individual response to a general crisis. The solitary reader engages with the disembodied writer in a world they create together. But the wider confusion of the public and the private remains, and grows unabated, leaving us to make our lives in a wider culture that treats the stuff of life ever more inadequately. Literary culture becomes ever more beleaguered, as writers and their readers huddle closer in the shrinking spaces they share. The achievements of writers and readers are real, but they help make bearable something that we should instead endeavour to change. Something similar can be said of the more responsible strands of therapeutic culture. Suffering can be relieved, and much can be done to help us deal with what has happened in the past and with the dilemmas we now face. But there is surely something wrong if even an ordinary unhappiness costs more than most people can afford. Certainly there are few of us who wouldn't benefit from some time spent talking in confidence with a qualified professional, but all of us would benefit from talking with one another about matters of common concern.

A purely private project to come to terms with the world cannot offer much hope of an escape from private distress. Some of us take refuge in intimate life, using the resources of literature and therapy as well as human affection to offset a working culture that grows ever more hostile to ordinary human virtues. Those who dissent openly from the governing ideology do not, it is fair to say, tend to flourish. Indeed, the near-perfect correlation of acceptance of the status quo and career advancement discourages most of us from straying into areas where our activities might upset our employers. In the absence of public institutions where collective responses to structural problems can be developed the individual is left alone in a horribly uneven struggle with those who currently control the terms of debate and the systems of description. Those who resist can be easily become demoralized and depressed when the dominant culture explains resistance in terms of psychological flaws or evolutionary unfitness.

Changes to the constitution of the self cannot be expected to deal with the causes of a crisis that, though often experienced as private unhappiness, has its origins in the structure of our governing institutions, which are also a collection of interlocking and reinforcing descriptions of what is natural and unnatural, inevitable and impossible, rational and unhinged. The assumptions that determine the limits of political discussion can only be challenged effectively through public action. In the final section of the book I outline the changes needed if action of this kind is to become possible. We do not know the world; we do not know each other; we do not know ourselves. We cannot expect to escape this three-fold failure to understand given the current system of institutions and descriptions. It is time to build another.

PART 3

The Return of the Public

CHAPTER 10

Public Commissioning

How can you show esteem for a journalist who does his job well?
Pierre Bourdieu

S O FAR I have sketched the history of the idea of the public and set out some of the most influential ideas associated with it. I have shown how these ideas have played out in the last generation as a particular – our particular – crisis. This crisis reveals itself both in the structural inability of the institutions of modern society to describe reality accurately in a time-frame that permits reasoned decision-making about matters of common concern and in the distress caused by our lack of a factually adequate account of the world and hence of a public dimension to our lives.

In what follows I set out a response to this crisis that is also a programme of political reform. In it I concentrate on changes that might be made to the structure of our institutions. In other words, my intention is not to urge individuals working in existing institutions to try harder to make the current arrangements work.

For most employees, most of the time, enlightened virtue, in the sense of a disinterested commitment to universal principles of truth and justice, is an unaffordable luxury. As we attempt to build our careers in hierarchical institutions we are forced to decide between the abnegation of the public self and private disaster. As a consequence, we live with a permanent dissonance between what we are required to believe about the world in order to remain socially viable and what, with some effort, we can piece together about how things are in fact. In these circumstances knowledge has an ambiguous quality. While enlightened rhetoric insists that it is good to know, and to share that knowledge, disinterested inquiry can rapidly take us very far away from the conventions that shape daily life for most people. To exhort people to make the effort required to become informed without changing the system of communication makes no sense; it amounts to demanding that we work harder to acquaint ourselves with our inability to convert knowledge of current conditions into political change. This strain of reformism takes on a properly Sadean quality since it offers the general spectacle of vice rewarded and virtue punished, and forces each of us to choose between hypocrisy and self-destruction.

Since a clear understanding of the world invariably serves to estrange us from it, it is tempting for those who aspire to effective action in the world to conclude that the majority is incapable of reason. As the ambitious dispense with democratic values they embrace instead the consoling dramas offered by the culture industry in which the achievements of an allegedly enlightened modernity face imminent destruction. These stories, so appealing to the self-regard of intellectuals and so useful to the ruling powers, saturate much of what passes for an attempt to describe current conditions. Better by far to berate the ignorant foot soldiers of the Christian right and to luxuriate in the shortcomings of the ontological argument than to explore the connections between faith, money, crime and state power; better to blame the poor for their predicament than to examine the structural causes of extreme inequality; better to worry over the antics of alternative therapists than to examine the scandals of modern medicine. In this way much of what passes for intellectual life in Anglo-America promises the sensation of reasoned and passionate engagement with the times in which we live while ignoring those facts that touch on the distribution of power.

There is only so much that we can do as individuals and

self-organizing groups about this and other forms of mystification. New technology enables us to access vast amounts of information very easily, and to communicate with others. The internet makes it easier for the individual to piece together a world-view that runs counter to those offered by the mainstream sources of information. But the mainstream remains the mainstream. Information cannot reliably reach a general audience without passing through some kind of editorial filter. Such filtering remains, to a very large extent, beyond the reach of general scrutiny and impervious to revision or appeal, since the general population is rarely aware of the decisions of editors. Most of us depend on institutions that we do not understand in our attempts to understand the world. Even when quite large numbers of people are able to develop an alternative analysis to that offered by the mainstream media, the latest financial crisis has shown that such painstaking, often unpaid, work can be ignored or ridiculed until it is too late to avert disaster. Maintaining a commitment to independent inquiry may be admirable, but personal virtue will not suffice. As Christopher Lasch puts it, 'in the absence of democratic exchange most people lack the incentive to master the knowledge that would make them capable citizens.'[1]

Kant thought that Enlightenment only becomes possible when we are able to reason and to communicate outside the confines of private institutions, including the state. Once liberated from our duties of loyalty we can reason freely and share our reasoning with others, in the manner of scholars before a reading public. Institutions can never provide a public space in Kant's sense of the word. But at present the most-watched and most-read sources of information do not provide the raw material – accurate information – on which public reason might draw. Nor do the current institutions make it possible to share the findings of disinterested reason with a wide audience. Only those who have an established private status (in Kant's sense of the word private) can gain reliable access to publicity, on the grounds that they represent legitimate interests or that they possess the relevant expertise. We do not have adequate means to form our own opinions, and have to rely on what Kant would call private institutions to create them for us. What we call public opinion takes much of its form from, and hence is substantially the instrument of, private interests. In short, we cannot assert ourselves as public beings, given the current means of communication.

What I am proposing then, is not a revolution or a utopia so much as a process that, beginning with minor reforms to the structure of media provision, will lead to further reforms. The constitution of information and ideas is the point on which to concentrate, since a world understood by the majority of citizens in a state is a world that stands ready to be transformed. In a world so understood, as the Machiavelli of *The Prince* recognized with a shudder, 'one change always leaves a toothing stone (*adentellato*) for the next'. Each element of a reform of the constitution of communication provides the means to establish the next, as if it were a section of a wall with 'a projection . . . to provide for its continuation'.[2] As the field of publicity changes, opinion changes. As opinion changes so too does the scope of the political.

The first reform is modest and possible. Indeed I almost hope that its significance will go unnoticed. But once achieved it makes the next, less modest, change much more difficult to resist, and so on, until as reasoning individuals we are able to secure control over the means by which public opinion is produced, with all that that implies for the current order of understanding and distribution of power. A well-informed citizenry will only establish itself if knowledge of the world connects reliably with the power to change it. For this to happen our knowledge must have a public dimension in two senses. It must be secured in part by collective action and it must be widely shared with others.

It may be exciting and heartening to talk of a global multitude or of the coming insurrection. But it is surely better to focus on the creation of an autonomous public opinion, since the majority in society can only exercise sovereign control once it has access to reliable information about the world and itself, once it has constituted itself as a public. Whatever ever else one wishes to change, a reformed system of information provides the only hope to securing that change by democratically legitimate means. Similarly, it is always tempting to appeal to existing decision-makers to make changes that are in the common interest, that are rationally justifiable. But efforts at reform or transformation stand or fall on the basis of the pictures that most people carry in their heads about what is possible, necessary and just. Those who currently control powerful state and corporate institutions will find rational grounds for action once an informed public is on hand to encourage or compel them to do so.

This is not to propose the sweeping away of existing media forms. Rather, the aim must be supplement them with new institutions of information. At present commissioning editors working either for companies or for state broadcasters hold a near monopoly on both the investigative agenda and the publicity given to information. Without their support, journalists cannot usually find the material means to investigate stories. Even when they do bypass the existing commissioning process, either by accessing foundation funding or by using their own resources (as in 'citizen journalism'), they can usually only reach a mass audience if decision-makers in the conventional media consent to broadcast their findings. Sometimes information discovered by independent researchers can find its way into mainstream news coverage, but the process is by no means automatic. The most important single investigative journalist in Britain, Heather Brooke, worked for years to make the public aware of the misuse of state funds by MPs. But the scandal only broke when the *Daily Telegraph* took the decision to publish the details of expenses claims. The credibility of stories and their news value continue to be determined by individuals who are directly accountable to their institutional superiors but are not subject to a more general scrutiny. The recent, and very serious, failures of the media make it clear that the civic spirit of public journalism, the participatory zeal of citizen journalism, and the resources of digital technology do not suffice to establish a widely shared account of the world that corresponds with the facts and that can therefore provide the basis for properly public decision-making.

My first proposal, therefore, is that a public commissioning system be established to run alongside the existing public service and commercial broadcasters and publishers. In this system citizens would, collectively and equally, make decisions about the allocation of resources to journalists and researchers. Each of us would be able to provide a certain amount of material support for projects that we wanted to see funded according to an agreed formula. This formula would include a minimum number of votes to support a given amount of funding, and votes could be split to support a number of projects according to an expressed set of priorities. The details of this formula hold the potential for a tremendous amount of mischief, of course; but the principle is clear. Each citizen should have an equal say in how public money is used to support journalism in the public interest. There is no need for a separate group of editorial decision-makers to stand between the commissioning audience and the investigating journalist.

Public commissioning of this kind would provide a venue, and a reason, for common deliberation. This would enable us to address current conditions of steepening inequality and deepening social distress in at least three ways. First, it would widen the realm of civic equality, in which market relations are suspended or heavily qualified, and allow individuals otherwise silenced or excluded to address others on matters of common concern as fellow citizens. This in turn would promote what the Athenians thought most valuable and distinctive about their constitution: the experience of *isonomia*, equality under the law.

Second, civic action in conditions of equality – the process of securing greater popular control over the climate of opinion – will make further participation seem less daunting or pointless. In this sense democratic commissioning will lend substance to Dewey's notion of a 'Great Community', in which conversation between equals provides the means to comprehend the impersonal systems of modern power. The practice of debate and deliberation, and the experience of changing the field of publicity, itself emboldens, since, as Aristotle pointed out, 'we are what we repeatedly do'. The mechanisms of public commissioning could therefore be expected to provide us all with an education in modes of collective self-government. Not only that, the very uneven distribution of the power to describe constitutes an important source of distress. Social disparagement takes place through images and stories, and public commissioning would give everyone the power to challenge the claims made about minorities, women, the young, or the poor.

Third, and most importantly, by giving the general population the means to inquire into the nature of social arrangements, public commissioning could provide the facts, and the publicity for those facts, that constitute the only sure basis for political change. Public commissioning could be a device for exploring the causes and consequences of inequality and injustice and for discovering and applying the remedies. We would be motivated to act because the information uncovered could be expected to reach the public-as-audience and hence to inform the shared sense of what was both politically possible and morally necessary. The exercise of power in order to secure individual freedom serves as an inducement for everyone to participate.

To fund this system of public commissioning a sum of money could be taken from tax revenues or from licence fees and allocated to trusts. Journalists, academics and citizen researchers would post proposals for funding with these trusts. These proposals would be made available online and in print in municipal libraries and elsewhere. Applicants would outline the purposes of the inquiry, the time frame and the resources needed. The public would then vote for the proposals that it wanted to support. These proposals might range from the hyper-local to the transnational in scope. Each citizen would have the same power to allocate resources. Each round of voting would be preceded by a series of public meetings, at which those seeking support would be free to make their case and to answer questions from the interested population. Those pitching for funds would make the case for the investigations they wanted to conduct, giving as much detail as they thought consistent with their objectives. These formal presentations could be supplemented by meetings of 'unofficial publics' where those seeking to raise awareness of particular concerns might prepare proposals. Meetings would also be held to discuss the content of reports once they are completed and to assess the prominence they should be given in subsequent forms of publication.

The results of inquiries could also be made available to commercial and state-owned broadcasters and publishers. But the public that commissioned the stories would also determine how much and what kinds of publicity each received in the channels of communication it controlled. The key point would be that the decision to investigate, and the decision to publicize the findings of investigations, would no longer be in the power of employers or of private owners. Instead the general population would decide on the basis of a series of votes. In this way, the means would finally be made available for individuals to initiate investigations that touch on matters of deep general concern but that cannot secure support in the existing commissioning institutions.

This is not to be confused with 'public journalism', which encourages professional journalists working in the established framework of institutions to become more civic-minded and to see their role as one of 'forming, as well as informing', the public.[3] While it might be flattering for journalists to imagine that they can reform the media simply by adopting more rigorous professional standards, they do not have the independence necessary to escape the constraints established by their owners. J. A. Hobson had the measure of editorial independence back in 1901 when he wrote, in the context of the Boer War:

> Mr Garrett is indignant when the impartiality and independence
> of his position have been called into question: he has had an abso-
> lutely free hand and this was a condition of his employment. The
> same is the case with Mr Moneypenny . . . What is the real worth
> of the protestations of these gentlemen? The answer is plain.
> When these editors were appointed, it was ascertained that they
> favoured the policy of the proprietors, and that they would likely
> work vigorously along the desired lines; if they departed from
> those lines they would be dismissed from their post and other
> editors appointed who would write what was wanted.[4]

The point extends to editors in state-owned media groups, of course.
Advancement in the BBC, for example, depends on application and
talent, but it can always be halted when journalists lose sight, or fail
to register, the limits of acceptable controversy. In the David Kelly
affair, for example, the journalist Andrew Gilligan, the Director
General of the BBC, Greg Dyke, and the Chairman of its Board of
Governors, Gavyn Davies, all lost their jobs when Gilligan's reporting raised questions about the government's use of intelligence in the
run-up to the invasion of Iraq. David Kelly himself lost a good deal
more than his job, of course, in circumstances that remain deeply
troubling. In the normal course of events, journalists sincerely
believe that they are free to report the truth as they see fit up until
the moment when they discover that they are not. Like Mr Garrett
and Mr Moneypenny, even the most confidently free-spirited editors
and journalists must remain committed to a world-view that dove-
tails with the needs of the institutions for which they work.

'Public journalism' thus leaves the existing structure of power
untouched and unexamined. It encourages journalists to think of
themselves as objective professionals who need only try harder.
Meanwhile they continue to operate in conditions set by editors,
while the editors continue to depend on owners – or their superiors

in the bureaucratic or political hierarchy – for their status and for their livelihood. It is as well to recall Harrington's point, that 'he who wants bread is his servant that will feed him'.[5] The institutional logics of the state and the corporation dominate the structure of decision-making in the media, and 'public journalism' of the sort lavishly promoted by foundations in the United States doesn't change that.

Public commissioning, as opposed to public journalism, replaces the power of owners and superiors with the power of citizens at crucial points of decision. But it is not the same as citizen journalism. Journalists working to public commissions can hope to build careers by addressing matters of common concern; they can specialize, they can develop a deep understanding of their subject and build stable networks of sources; they will not be subject to simple veto or more subtle forms of coercion from their employers; they will be more directly answerable to the audiences they serve. This does not remove the division of labour, but it does put expertise at the service of the eventual audience for journalism. Public commissioning will hopefully invigorate citizen journalism by providing non-professional journalists with access to funds. But it will do so while also providing full-time journalists with a material alternative to existing patron-client relationships. Professional journalists who come under intolerable pressure, or whose lines of inquiry lead them into conflict with their employers, can move to a parallel system of commissioning. And the funds will also be available to engaged professionals and academics who want to produce reports for the general readers.

A proposal very similar to public commissioning has been set out in the United States. Drawing on the ideas of Dean and Randy Baker, John Nichols and Robert McChesney have suggested that each citizen be given a 'Citizenship News Voucher' that they can use annually to support media institutions. Everyone would have the same value voucher, which could be split between organizations or left unused.[6] Such a reform would be a huge step towards a democratically accountable media but it falls short of establishing a direct relationship between the public-as-commissioner and the journalist-as-agent. By supporting publishing institutions a voucher system leaves commissioning decisions in the hands of media professionals, even if those professionals are motivated to pay closer attention to the views of the public that support them. If they are operating with a mix of voucher funding and advertising support this might tend to affect their editorial judgement.

Media professionals, even those with the best will in the world, cannot be left to determine what constitutes public interest journalism; it is a matter for the public. Public commissioning could be used to provide funds for media institutions, of course. But it could also be used to support journalism and research from independent individuals and from groups not primarily in the news business. The ability of everyone to make proposals for funding ensures that the media institutions themselves remain objects of effective scrutiny.[7]

Most importantly, the requirement that journalists set out the terms of the investigations they want to pursue promotes a discussion among citizens about the kinds of new information they would value. The citizen body comes into being through the conversation among equals; it is not the more or less idealised object of the professional editor's imaginings or calculations. Enormous effort goes into trying to figure out what the existing readership or audience of a particular publication will find engaging. The aim of public commissioning is not to satisfy defined demographics but to provide the conditions for a general transformation. The act of deliberation, as much as the eventual product of that deliberation, promotes this transformation by allowing us to orientate the private world of sentiment with the public world of fact.

The proposals for radical reform from McChesney and Nichols and myself imply that we reject the notion, still occasionally put forward, that the aggression and scepticism of the media needs to be reined in before it corrodes faith in democracy. I struggle to understand how anyone can imagine that journalism is too adversarial or sceptical about state power, big business or the finance sector. The scandals at Enron, World.com and elsewhere were only preludes, it now seems, to the awesome deficiencies of ordinary suspicion that characterized the journalism of the new century. While journalists at the *Wall Street Journal* and the *Financial Times* might want to assure their readers that no one could have known a major economic crisis was imminent, they are as unreliable now as they were befuddled then. Similarly, while politicians might continue to complain that the coverage they receive is often extremely unpleasant and unfair, in many instances they have been able to do as much they pleased since the population consistently lacked the information it needed to challenge them.

Most of those who relied on the major media did not know, and were not told, that neoliberal policies had established a pattern of wealth inequality, global trade imbalances and unregulated financial activity that made the recent collapse all but inevitable. Likewise, they did not know that mortgage lending in the United States had passed from wilful optimism into culpable, and often downright criminal, negligence. Plenty of people knew that trouble was brewing and did what they could to warn the rest of us. But for the most part the press ignored them.[8]

In Britain the population pays an annual licence to receive broadcast television. This fee raises some £3.4 billion annually.[9] The BBC currently sets aside 3.5 per cent of this to cover the costs of the transfer to digital provision. In 2009 the Labour government proposed that this 3.5 per cent of license fee revenue, amounting to around £120 million per year, be used to provide a replacement for commercial television's regional news service.[10] However, the head of Ofcom, Ed Richards, indicated that a 'straight replacement' for ITV regional news would cost between £40 and £60 million annually.[11] My proposal then, is that the balance of the money, some £80 million, should be controlled by the population as a whole, through a system of participatory commissioning. This would give the population enough money to pay the equivalent of 3,000 journalists and researchers a basic annual salary of £24,000 to work full-time on matters of interest and concern to the general population.

In the system of public commissioning I propose, Wales, Scotland, Northern Ireland, and each English region would have a statutory body that holds and disperses the funds to researchers and publishes the results. They would also organize open meetings at which applicants could make presentations and answer questions both before and after investigations. The companies providing regional news on the independent television networks could be mandated to publish the results of publicly funded research, according to priorities established by those active in the commissioning process and in the process of debate following each round of inquiry. Newspapers currently published by local government could also be required to carry stories, in line with a vote by the relevant publics. Where large-scale commercial operators or the BBC make extensive use of publicly generated material, they would be charged and the resulting income shared between the journalists and researchers responsible and the public commissioning bodies that sponsored their original work. Small-scale private publishers could use the same material at very low cost or for free. Publicly generated material would in this way support a rich network of community-run news outlets, employee-owned ventures and private start-ups.

There are currently between 75 and 100 full-time investigative journalists working in Britain.[12] They are all dependent on professional commissioning editors for their income and for their access to an audience. The system I propose would make it possible for the population to support around 250 full-time investigative journalists and researchers in each region and devolved nation. These journalists would be motivated not to please their editors but to build working bases of support for themselves. Some might concentrate on particular geographical areas, some on particular kinds of inquiry. But all would have a direct incentive to work closely with people who could provide support for their applications for further work. Reputations would be established on the basis of service to the general population. Investigative skills would migrate towards matters where substantial numbers of people expressed interest. Journalists working throughout Britain would have an opportunity to develop national and global, as well as regional, fields of expertise. National institutions, the EU and institutions like the International Monetary Fund, the World Bank and the Bank of International Settlements would all become available to sustained scrutiny from non-metropolitan researchers and their sponsoring audiences. Journalists working at a regional level would be able to follow a story nationally, transnationally and offshore. A controversy about local planning could be connected with investigations into national policy and the tax avoidance practices of large companies. By uncovering connections between the local, the regional and the global, public commissioning could help strengthen face-to-face publics by showing that there is nowhere that is not part of the wider world. The regional organization of the funding bodies would allow clusters of expertise to develop. Retired professionals could begin the work of mapping the imaginary spaces of the offshore world; doctors could develop research programmes that were also experiments in new forms of civic life.

It might be argued that the population will allocate money to journalists who promise to pursue popular lines of inquiry – in other words, that public commissioning will end up supporting the kinds of journalism that are already commercially successful. But I doubt that people will commission material they know the current media system already delivers very efficiently. Many people may currently pay for gossip about celebrity or public figures, but I suspect that their priorities would change if they were commissioning journalism for themselves. Once the operations of the state and other powerful institutions, including the media, become available as objects of unblinking scrutiny, they will become the focus of at least some commissioning. And even if we are as morally degraded as the most cynical tabloid editor, the existing protections from invasions of privacy and libel would remain in place.[13] Prurience and moral panics are matters of impulse, at least as far as audiences as concerned. At present, editors in commercial organizations exercise considerable ingenuity in stirring up popular fear and distrust. All the tricks of selective quotation and framing go into the sensational reporting of both crime and social change. But I cannot see the population scheduling, and then paying directly for, bouts of ill-informed outrage.

Some might object that fascist or other groups would seize on public commissioning and use it to spread distorted information or outright untruths. But this objection presupposes that the existing media don't already seek to inflame commercially useful hatreds. It is clear, for example, that the current climate of hostility towards Muslims in Britain has been driven more by mainstream journalism and politics than by avowedly fascist agitation.[14] Public commissioning would allow Muslims to respond effectively to the way they are represented in the press and to promote wider awareness of the discrimination, abuse and violence they experience. At present the media indulge in stereotype and caricature more or less at will. Public commissioning would establish an effective means by which targeted groups might respond and build links with the wider society.

Similarly, some might want to dismiss the idea of public commissioning on the grounds that it will favour the articulate and privileged. However, since commissioning is already currently the sole preserve of privileged and articulate elites, a system where individuals enjoy equal power to shape the investigative agenda can hardly be rejected on these grounds on the basis of mere supposition. Indeed, public commissioning might tend to favour those who – like the retired and the long-term unemployed – have the time to examine proposals in detail and who will be motivated to collaborate in changing the field of publicity.

A similar system of public commissioning could be established in the United States, without doing any damage to the principles of private property or troubling those who continue to believe in the liberating power of the free market. In 1934 the Roosevelt administration established the terms on which radio (and later television) broadcasters would operate. Roosevelt granted broadcasters access to the airwaves but required that they submit to regulation by a government agency, the Federal Communications Commission (FCC). This commission was given wide-ranging powers to take action as 'public convenience, interest, or necessity requires'.[15] The New Deal Democrats acted as they did on the grounds that the public owned the airwaves that provided the media companies with their opportunities to make money. This principle has been restated regularly by American politicians but rarely asserted in fact. In his 1998 State of the Union address, President Clinton indicated that he wanted to address the cause of spiralling campaign costs – 'the high cost of media advertising'. He would request that the FCC 'act to provide free or reduced cost television time for candidates' on the grounds that 'the airwaves are a public trust, and broadcasters have to help us in this effort to strengthen our democracy'.[16] Opposition in Congress, from Tom DeLay among others, ensured that the FCC did no such thing.[17]

If, as I contend, 'the public convenience, interest and necessity' require that the funds be raised to create a system of democratically controlled commissioning, there is no constitutional impediment to levying these funds from broadcasters in exchange for their right to make use of what are public assets. There is furthermore no obstacle to insisting that broadcasters make provision to publish the findings of publicly funded research, in accordance with the expressed desires of the relevant publics. If they were to pay a levy to support public commissioning and the infrastructure to publish the findings, the networks might in turn be freed from any obligation to produce news programmes themselves. They could be relieved of their onerous public service functions and could focus instead on producing entertainment. By removing the monopoly on broadcast news currently enjoyed by companies that depend on advertising revenue, public commissioning would move the news agenda closer to people's expressed concerns and allay the suspicion that broadcasters are too attentive to the needs of advertisers and other powerful interests.

I can see no serious objections to reform of the architecture of communications in the United States along these lines. As Michael Schudson and Leonard Downie point out, the American media have always enjoyed extensive state support. In the early years of the Republic the government subsidized newspapers sent in the mail, for example.[18] A levy on commercial broadcasters would provide the means by which an autonomous public opinion might be created. And that is, after all, nothing less than a precondition for democratic government. The broadcast frequencies do not belong to the media conglomerates that use them. Changing the terms on which they enjoy access to them has no implications for free speech or for the rights of private property. As currently constituted, the media in the United States do not provide the public with the resources it needs if it is to conduct itself as the animating interest in a democracy. It would be a matter of simple administration, rather than a revolution in the country's affairs, to remedy a situation that is only generally tolerated because it is generally unrecognized.

Once the principle is established, and the general population has begun to register the possibilities of a public system of newsgathering, more funds might be made available. Some of the funds from taxation that are currently used to support a centralized system of information management by state institutions could be placed under the direct control of regional and national publics. The money currently spent by the Pentagon on public relations – at least $4.7 billion according to the Associated Press – could be diverted into a system of public oversight of defence contracts and independent assessments of the country's military needs.[19] Money currently spent on public diplomacy and psychological warfare could be also be used to monitor the activities of the state and other powerful institutions in accordance with the expressed wishes of the population. In Britain too, the state's expenditure on information could be opened up to general scrutiny and media management and psychological warfare budgets could find their way into the public commissioning system. In time the communications resources of the state would be brought under democratic control and a system currently used to shape popular perceptions and insulate elite decision-making would give citizens some share in the creation of their own beliefs.

Of course, the system of publicly commissioned information could be made to engage with the electoral process. This could be done by giving citizens, whether organized as parties or not, the chance to distribute resources to political campaign communications. At the beginning of an election the public could vote for those they wanted to hear from – they could allocate support to groups that they think might have an interesting set of policies, or a worthwhile perspective on matters of common concern. Political parties and other groups in civil society – unions, NGOs, etc. – would then be given money and air time commensurate with the support expressed. Each commissioning group would form the primary audience for the material produced and would, presumably, seek to promote policies they agreed with more widely. In this way, candidates and groups in civil society who cannot currently establish their credibility in an information context dominated by established interests would be given opportunities to reach an audience at the moment of decision and to address it in specifically political terms.[20]

The changes I propose here would have a major impact on the political culture of Britain and the United States. Rather than leaving the formation of public opinion in the exclusive control of the expert members of Lippmann's national system of knowledge, the population as a whole would have the means to bring new information to light, to share existing information, and to create descriptions of the world at every level to set against, and if necessary to challenge, those offered by powerful institutions. Any issue where there might be doubt over the prevailing consensus – for example the trade in illicit drugs, the struggle with terrorism, the global financial architecture, or the governing views on economic development, peace and war – could, in a system of public commissioning, be opened up to scrutiny made effectual by the democratic distribution of funds. Nothing that could secure the support of a public would be denied funds, subject only to the existing provisions of the law regarding libel, privacy and incitement. The popular understanding would then be limited only by the information available and the ingenuity of those commissioned to assemble and present it. In the course of a popularly mandated programme of inquiry, the general population would come to know more intimately both the necessary and the artificial limits of its knowledge. Commercial confidentiality, state secrecy and other forms of privacy would all become forms of visible and sharply delineated darkness, rather than the causes of a general dimming of vision.

As de Tocqueville pointed out, in a democracy public opinion is sovereign. But the sovereignty of public opinion is empty if the public cannot independently establish its own opinion. If, as at present, public opinion derives from the information a nationally organized system of insiders deign to make available, then 'public opinion' remains the creature of private interests. A few private actors dignify their own view of the world by seeing it reflected in the real or imagined beliefs of the population at large. This remains true even when those who control the flow of information are well-meaning and professional, as many of those in the communications business doubtless are. At crucial moments, and in crucial areas, the media cannot reliably provide us with the knowledge we need if we are both to govern ourselves and take part as adults in debates about matters of common concern. The media demonstrably fail to describe the world accurately, telling us stories about human nature and motivation that are no less deceptive for being partly true. And then they sell us cures for the resulting distress that do not and cannot work.

In such circumstances the invigilating public of the liberal imagination does not exist. The major political parties compete for office in a determinedly private register. Candidates are sold on the basis of their personal character, their competence, and the emotional responses they can inspire or provoke. The brand associations of abstract nouns replace political programmes while the language of morality and values replaces a clear account of what politicians intend to do.[21] The media take direction from networks constituted by the interlinked institutions of state and private power. If, as Hume argued, opinion underpins government in the widest sense, then the media are inextricably political in nature. In current circumstances it is absurd to call on journalists to try harder to be civic-minded and responsible since by definition they must take into account existing patterns of power. To be powerful is to influence the field of publicity. Only changes in the distribution of power in the media can therefore make journalism serve the general population more reliably.

Advocates of the market system of news provision argue that competition allows truth to drive out error. But the concentration of ownership, the dependence on the profit motive, and the shared interests of media owners and other powerful institutions and groups mean that the coverage of matters of fundamental importance cannot suffice. On the other hand, the supporters of public service provision claim that disinterested experts can provide a framework for rational civic engagement by offering a balanced account of controversial matters. It would be nice to think that wealthy foundations or state bureaucracies could live up to their billings as disinterested patrons of fearless reporting. Yet here too, unaccountable power relations, not to mention the class affiliations of media professionals, mean that crucial facts will always escape adequate investigation in institutions run by state employees or the beneficiaries of philanthropic support. The demonstrable failures of both liberal market and public service models of news provision make it necessary to create something new. The innovation suggested here reverts to a tradition of freedom that predates both liberalism and the ethic of public service. Public commissioning, like the early republicans, recognizes that a sovereign public can only establish itself under conditions of general participation.

To repeat, this is not to advocate citizen journalism of the sort that currently excites so much interest and attention. Citizens need to take direct control of material resources and distribute them at the point of commissioning and at the point of publication. The news-gathering itself can remain a task mostly undertaken by professionals, so long as the population directs their work on the basis of a vote and so long as the salience given to this work is determined by general deliberation. Public commissioning generates new kinds of knowledge by establishing a new mechanism for bringing information to light and making it widely known. This generally shared account of the world is a commonly managed resource that sustains democratic power by creating informed and mutually aware citizens. Citizens have the means to change this generally shared account by directing journalistic curiosity and by highlighting discoveries they consider important. The Republic begins in a commonwealth of descriptions.

The institutions established to enable public commissioning do not constitute a space for deliberation that is straightforwardly public in Kant's sense of the word. Every institution is a private body, in the same way that a church congregation is private. Similarly, those seeking public funds will be private actors in the sense that they will depend on the goodwill of a superior (in this case a voting public) for their well-being. The vices of the court will still exist when the general population is sovereign. But public commissioning will provide the means by which an actually existing public, a public of individuals who are able to act outside the constraints imposed on them in their working life, might come to approximate the ideal public of a disinterested group of scholars. Not because we can expect suddenly to be overcome by a virtuous desire for truth, but because we already love the truth, when our own self-love and self-interest do not seem to be threatened. Public commissioning along the lines I have sketched allows us to examine critically the governing descriptions of political economy in its broadest sense. It gives us the means to talk back effectively to the existing powers by challenging their claims in the minds of our peers. And it gives us a factual basis on which to reason in the general interest. Furthermore, public commissioning as an approach to media reform in regional and national contexts gives us the opportunity, should be wish to take it, to reason as members of a global civil society.

Most of us would prefer to live in a just world than an unjust one, and we would all prefer to rely on accurate descriptions of the world than on fantastical ones. Injustice must base itself on lies. A reformed method for finding out about the world is a precondition for changing it. Certainly we are guilty of injustice and mendacity; and we are all subject to the gravity of self-interest. But for all that we fear to face certain facts about ourselves and the world, and for all our habits of self-deception, we do not want to be deceived. We continue to want to live in a world safe for, or less lethal to, true descriptions. Public commissioning does not by any means offer us the prospect of a world without error. But it points the way to another world, nonetheless.

CHAPTER ELEVEN

A Public System of Knowledge

Oh, how much today is hidden by science! Oh, how much it is expected to hide!

Friedrich Nietzsche

T HE BREAKDOWN IN our system of knowledge extends far beyond the day-to-day of print and broadcast journalism to include much of academia, including the most prestigious and influential of the social sciences, economics. As Joseph Stiglitz has pointed out, 'if science is defined by its ability to forecast the future, the failure of much of the economics profession to see the crisis coming should be a cause of great concern'. Stiglitz himself thinks that this widespread failure has led to 'deep reflection' on the part of professional economists.[1] Perhaps this is so. But its failures of description and prediction should cause us to think much more carefully about the institutional basis of research in the social sciences, the distribution of resources and status between disciplines, and the formal and informal constraints within which academics currently work. As the financier turned reformer Philip Augar has pointed out, over the course of a generation 'finance wrapped its tentacles around the relevant parts of the academic world . . . under these circumstances it is little wonder that so much academic output was supportive of the financial system'.[2] The content of crucial disciplines moulded itself to the needs of powerful institutions and media coverage reflected the facts of social power by highlighting the views of researchers whose work assisted the state and the corporation. As the preamble to the financial crisis shows, powerful interests in the conjoined worlds of finance and the media have treated economists as resources that they could commission and publicize at will.

At times the state intervenes on the grand scale to eliminate styles of thought that present problems for it. The wave of intimidation associated with Joseph McCarthy cleared the universities of those scholars whose work did not sit well with the Cold War system of knowledge and encouraged those who remained to make themselves useful in the struggle against Soviet totalitarianism. Of course many academics and their conservative critics like to think of themselves as dangerous radicals, but the traditions of radicalism still extant in the universities and the career paths they create are what were left once the work of national coordination took place in the early years of the Cold War. Aside from occasional campaigns against individual academics and disciplines, the operations of the academic labour market help ensure a degree of conformity. The exhilaration of professional success and the gravity of failure elevate those willing to work within the bounds of legitimate controversy and wear down those whose curiosity takes them in unhelpful directions. The current system of publicity leaves these processes and their implications opaque.

In the United States, private foundations established by industrialists in the early years of the twentieth century have to a considerable extent shaped academic disciplines and allocated prestige within and between them, in line with what Donald Fischer has called 'an ideology of sophisticated conservatism'.[3] In the 1920s and 1930s the Rockefeller foundations funded the United States Social Science Research Council and exercised enormous but largely invisible influence over the development of economics, psychology and sociology. In 1928 Harold Laski complained that 'it is merely the fact that a fund is in reach which permeates everything. The college develops along the lines the foundation approves. The dependence is merely implicit, but it is in fact quite final.'[4] The impact of the foundations was particularly profound, and particularly difficult to appreciate in hindsight, in the study of communications. Their funding helped tilt the discipline away from Dewey and towards Lippmann. The idea of communication as an opportunity to change others' views and to have one's own changed through conversation gave way to a transitive model, in which active and qualified experts adjusted the beliefs of passive audiences.[5]

In such circumstances it is hardly surprising that, as the critic and media analyst Herbert Schiller once remarked, social science has managed for the most part to ignore 'the most important fact about the last century . . . the global triumph of corporate capitalism'.[6] Not only that, in the social sciences broadly defined, prestige and status, and hence reliable access to publicity, have become almost completely detached from performance. As Henry Kissinger observed, expert status belongs to those who can elaborate and define the consensus of a 'constituency'.[7]

As long as the population cannot function as a constituency, expert status will not depend on providing accurate descriptions and predictions to a general audience but on serving undisclosed constituencies. Accordingly, economists on the margins who predicted the problems in the credit markets remain marginal while those who predicted a rosy future for self-regulation and free markets remain at the centre of decision-making and continue to dominate the debate about what to do next. The public have no means to assign expert status and publicity to those social scientists whose work had demonstrable predictive power, while unaccountable interests continue to puff the reputations of those they favour. It is, by way of analogy, as though physics remained dominated by papal patronage and career success depended on denouncing both Newton and Einstein.

That said, the flaws in the organization of physical science are also extremely serious. Here too, special interests including the state suppress accurate descriptions of the world and promote false ones

– the scientists responsible for discovering the health risks of asbestos and lead, Irving Selikoff and Herbert Needleman, both suffered from prolonged efforts to discredit them.[8] But more fundamentally the population as a whole has had almost no role in choosing the projects that have absorbed the talent and ingenuity of working scientists and the material resources on which they depend. There has been little or no open debate about what science is for, even though as taxpayers we are collectively the patrons of state-funded science. The imperatives of weapons research and product development have steered basic scientific training as well as advanced scientific practice towards areas that promise gains for state and corporate power. The full extent of what is missed in this particular distribution of curiosity can only be guessed at since, as the terrifying politician-administrator Donald Rumsfeld once pointed out, we do not always know what we don't know.

Harvey Brooks, a luminary in the liberal administration of science in the United States the 1960s, explained in *The Government of Science* that the 2 per cent of GDP the government spent on scientific research and development had 'disproportionate social and economic leverage, since the whole thrust of the economy is determined by scientific and technical research'.[9] Brooks argued that the American state became a major patron of science when it realized that 'the successful technical effort of the war years had drawn heavily on the bank of basic knowledge and research skills'.[10] Successive American administrations have channelled funds to basic science, as well as to technologies drawn from that science, to ensure that the state continues to have access to war-winning technology. Accordingly, the federal government provides most of the funding for basic science research in American universities. For example, four government agencies, the Department of Energy, the National Science Foundation, the Department of Defense and NASA support most of the research in physics.[11]

In 2004 the Department of Defense directly controlled around half of all state funding for scientific research and development, a staggering $62.8 billion.[12] And the distinction betweeen military and civilian funds is more apparent than real; the National Science Technology Council works to 'orient science and technology toward achieving national goals'. The council's members include the Secretary of Defense and the heads of NASA, the CIA and the National Institutes of Health. Though money may come from the National Science Foundation or the Department of Energy, they will have conferred with the military and intelligence agencies on the broad objectives of science research before final decisions are made. Again, the public has no direct access to the debate about what constitute 'national goals'. The heads of the military-industrial bureaucracy are left to decide.

As well as providing the military with a bank of basic knowledge and thence access to advanced technology, government spending in the defence sector also delivers mouth-watering profits to private industry. The more ambitious the US state becomes, the greater the scope for corporate gain. Now that the stated aim of the Pentagon is to maintain global military supremacy or 'full spectrum dominance',[13] the commercial opportunities are apparently limitless. Through defence contracting a handful of corporations secure vast sums from the US taxpayer. The 2010 defence budget has been set at $664 billion, about a fifth of total federal spending. Something in the region of $200 billion will be spent on military contracts, much of it on the hi-tech products of the major arms companies. And money doesn't always pass from the taxpayer to the Pentagon to the corporate sector in an orderly fashion. Sometimes it simply disappears. Speaking in 2001 the then Defense Secretary Donald Rumsfeld told his colleagues that 'according to some estimates we cannot track $2.3 trillion in transactions'.[14] That $2.3 trillion has all the hallmarks of a magic number; the Pentagon has no real idea how much money is being diverted fraudulently to powerful private interests. The emphasis on homeland security has only widened the scope for collusion between government employees and private companies and added large numbers of former intelligence operatives to the mix of politicians, lobbyists and retired soldiers who have grown rich in the tangles of the military-industrial complex.[15] All in all, the opportunities for straightforward profit and outright larceny are a permanent temptation, a temptation that arms manufacturers and mercenaries are not by their nature especially likely to resist.

The American state and the media are a little reticent as to why they want to maintain this terrifying military establishment. The Pentagon only rarely acknowledges that Americans who invest their money outside the United States deserve special consideration; the authors of Space Command's 'Vision for 2020' note, a little coyly, that 'historically, military forces have evolved to protect national interests and investments – both military and economic'.[16] Moreover the money spent on defence currently delivers massive profits to private interests and shapes technological development in ways that are consistent with the existing distribution of domestic power. Indeed military investment in computing has helped to consolidate corporate and financial power by allowing employers to replace millions of workers with software.

Electronics is only one sector where strategic investment by the state has provided an irreplaceable subsidy to particular forms of business. Much of the technical base of consumer capitalism depends on work originally commissioned by the US state. In this way, as Brooks acknowledged, the state and its corporate collaborators continue to determine 'the whole thrust of the economy'. Not surprisingly, the state and the corporations push the economy in directions that enhance their power and the power of those who control them, relative to both real and imagined threats. The state extracts money from the population in the form of taxation and uses it to create technology that only occasionally and accidentally contributes to the general good. More often defence technologies feed into the civilian economy in ways that tip the balance of power from workers to owners and from small to large companies. State expenditure transforms competition in the private economy, and technology developed for military use filters into the civilian economy at a pace and in forms that suit the companies that control it. As one might predict, this drip of military technology makes society more suspicious and more dangerous.[17]

An elaborate system of management helps scientists working for the government to maintain their self-image as autonomous seekers after truth. Most of them are reluctant to admit that their sponsors exert any influence over the work they do. Indeed it is important for them to believe that they act on their own initiative. The physicist Jeff Schmidt has detailed how academic researchers seeking funds from government agencies are encouraged to present unsolicited proposals. The agencies make their research needs known, they make it clear that only a fraction of the proposals they receive will be successful, and they encourage applicants to discuss their plans with in-house scientists. Given that writing a proposal is a time-consuming process, scientists tend to focus their efforts on areas where they believe that funds will be available. They don't have to choose areas that don't interest them, they just have to put aside areas that do interest them but that won't appeal to potential funders. As a scientist's career progresses, the expertise developed through intensive work in areas of interest to those who control research funds will make him or her ever more qualified to explore, and ever more personally invested in, those areas.[18]

Though the military establishment in Britain is far smaller than in the United States, the sums it spends are still highly significant. In 2003–4 the military directly controlled around 30 per cent of the state's total budget for research and development, some £2.7 billion. In the same year the military spent an estimated £6 billion on equipment. Military support for research and development and the purchase of materiel together do much to subsidize the remnants of the country's advanced manufacturing base. While our political leaders are full of praise for the free enterprise system, defence and security provide an ongoing rationale for largely unaccountable state intervention in the economy. The emphasis on weapons production ensures that Britain remains a major player in the international arms trade, with all that that implies in terms of state criminality. Note that the profits from this international trade find their way into private pockets, while the taxpayers of both the producing and the purchasing countries bear the costs.

The British state channels funds for research and development to corporations in other favoured sectors. For example, under a formula negotiated with the government in 2004, 28 per cent of the receipts from sales of branded drugs to the National Health Service were allocated to support the drug companies' research and development work.[19] The subsidy was worth between £2 and £3 billion annually. By way of comparison, according to the then Minister of State for Public Health, Gillian Merron, direct government funding for health research in 2009–10 came in at around £1.6 billion.[20] The UK government has been giving significantly more money to pharmaceutical corporations to spend on research and development than to its own health research agencies.

The results of this gigantic taxpayer subsidy have not been overwhelmingly impressive. For example, one of the big growth areas in pharmaceutical medicine has been the treatment of mental distress. Though the drug companies have come up with persuasive stories to justify a bewildering range of psychiatric drugs, there is little reason to take them seriously. Drugs they have to claimed to be safe, non-addictive, and effective have turned out to be dangerous, addictive and only marginally more effective than a placebo. Indeed some psychologists have suggested the drugs 'work' not by rectifying an imbalance in the brain's chemistry but by convincing some patients that, because they feel dizzy or agitated, they must be getting better; Prozac and a generation of miracle cures are effectively super-placebos.[21]

These drugs have been used to treat an epidemic of mental distress whose causes have barely been researched but that coincided with steep increases in inequality. They provided doctors with a response to the problems caused by social crisis that left the latter largely unexamined. More generally, drug companies have been endlessly inventive when it comes to drugs that imitate existing blockbusters; they have introduced a number of new treatments for pattern baldness, obesity and impotence. But their business model depends on their being able to patent legally novel chemical compounds that promise to become commercially viable product lines. This makes it difficult for them to focus on either preventing serious disease or curing it outright, given that the profit motive steers them towards chronic treatments for conditions found in large, affluent populations. The golden age of the pharmaceutical model of medical research is long past and only strenuous lobbying has kept the subsidies flowing.

Yet despite the patchy record of the pharmaceutical sector in delivering general benefits, researchers employed directly by the state work in an increasingly commercial environment. In recent years the state's support for science in Britain has been tied explicitly to market-oriented goals. The Medical Research Council, for example, is mandated to promote 'economic competitiveness' alongside its other duties. In practice this means that the pharmaceutical sector's assumptions about the goals for research predominate and the drive to develop lucrative patents exerts ever more influence on the minds of policy-makers, civil servants and researchers. The pharmaceutical industry's efforts to maintain a favourable climate of opinion pervade the scientific establishment. If they are as good at what they do as I suspect they are, then their work will go unnoticed by researchers who will continue to pride themselves on their intellectual autonomy while thinking along lines that serve the pharmaceutical agenda. And, as with defence contracting, the financial benefits of this taxpayer subsidy tend to accrue to the 'men on the inside, working under conditions that are sound'.[22]

In one way or another a veil of corporate confidentiality and state secrecy obscures the way the scientific agenda is shaped, even though much of the money comes directly from the taxpayer. The technical complexity of the work and the self-image of scientists as autonomous seekers after truth render the operations of the state and financial power in the scientific process even more opaque. But the consequences can hardly be missed. At present, publicly funded science and technology research serves the interest of a gigantic, global military establishment, which in turn reassures the tiny minority of American and British citizens who hold extensive investments overseas. It subsidizes favoured elements in the private economy and supports the concentration of power in fewer and fewer hands. Brilliant scientists dedicate themselves to work that contributes to a social and environmental catastrophe. The mythology of defence keeps the population from challenging, let alone changing, this perverse state of affairs.

In the absence of effective scrutiny, popular resentment of state expenditure concentrates on transfers of wealth from the middle classes to the poor, rather than on transfers from the majority to a relative handful of insiders. To give some sense of the distortions that then play out in current systems of reporting, in 2009 the *Daily Mail* devoted 370 words to a story about a woman who had been found guilty of 'raking in nearly £24,000 in disability allowances over five years while playing regularly in ladies' darts tournaments'.[23] The Pentagon's lost $2.3 trillion given proportionate treatment would run as a 370-word article every day for 262,557 years.

This is not to say that the wider population receives no benefits from the current ordering of scientific research. Rather, these benefits are accidental by-products of a system designed to tether the nominally public pursuit of knowledge to the service of private advantage. Those involved in the management of science, as well as many working scientists, insist on its disinterested nature. But science is not and can never be disinterested in so far as its objectives are concerned. The decision to distribute funds in particular fields of study can never be a purely technical matter. Scientific assessments of what is likely to produce interesting or practical knowledge are inevitably alloyed with the desires of those who control the system to develop particular forms of knowledge and with them new resources of power. At present the military and intelligence institutions of the state and a sophisticated fraction of the corporate sector largely determine the development paths of both basic science and advanced technology.

A participatory public could begin by determining the objectives of some fraction of publicly funded science. The techniques developed from close attention to particular problems, the expertise that scientists come to possess over the course of their careers, and the technologies that emerge from basic science, are all currently conditioned by factors external to science. The key question is not whether science is to be exposed to external interests, but whose interests are to predominate. Scientists exercise considerable influence in framing their objectives, since they necessarily enjoy a privileged understanding of the current range of possibilities. Their claims about what is practicable inevitably influence the objectives set and hence the detailed distribution of resources. Public commissioning will not alter this. But science must always take place in a political context and deals will always have to be struck with those putting up the money. At present the general population gives considerable sums to science to support objectives on which it has not been consulted and over which it exercises no real oversight. Scientists conduct their work in partnership with state and corporate interests. Public relations experts try to convince them that their service is perfect freedom and that, besides, no alternative funding model is possible since the population is childishly fearful of change.

Scientists carve out opportunities to study problems that interest them in partnership with particular interests. The institutions on which they depend for their funding, their prestige and their self-respect work assiduously to direct their work into fields that promise some measurable advantage to those who currently control the process. Scientists are encouraged to believe that the public will prove even more capricious than their current patrons and that a physics shaped by the imperatives of nuclear weapons research is better than no physics at all. But while decisions about scientific objectives touch on issues of feasibility they are, as I say, finally political matters. A general public, working with technical and scientific advisors, is as qualified as politicians, businessmen and civil servants to establish what science is for. To give the public some power to set the scientific agenda does not mean the end of inquiry for its own sake. Indeed an even fitfully prudent public will recognize the need to make provision for a great deal more in the way of thoroughly unencumbered curiosity that the current system permits. Science is both a matter of patient progress on paths already surveyed and of forays in directions that cannot satisfy bureaucratic standards in advance. A sensibly designed system of public patronage would give scientists the opportunity to explore lines of inquiry that would be blocked in the current system.

The opening up of science to effective public scrutiny could build on the institutions created to administer the public commissioning of investigative research. Indeed it is to be hoped that public commissioning of journalism would provide the public with the information it needs if it is to appreciate the problems with the current scientific establishment and to develop a viable alternative. As with the media, the process of reform should begin with a sum of money, and expand as the publics that congregate around this money become competent to manage larger sums.[24] In time, under conditions of general scrutiny, the subsidies enjoyed by private interests could be redirected to serve the common good. For example, as Dean Baker has suggested, the state could take direct responsibility for health research and cease to rely on pharmaceutical companies and their patent-protected drugs.[25] Private institutions would be free to develop new drugs but would no longer enjoy monopoly pricing power.

The public commissioning of science research could follow the approach outlined for media reform above. The regional bodies established to commission investigative journalism would add regular rounds of voting on proposals from scientists for funds. Scientists and researchers would submit proposals for research. It would be up to each public to determine the scope of proposals that they were willing to consider and to ensure that the money was spent wisely. The public could delegate their votes to expert groups that included individuals who would mediate between the scientific establishment and the general population. As with public commissioning in journalism, public patronage would create new institutions and career paths for individuals.

While scientists and researchers would be free to ask for further funds to develop drug therapies, they could also seek money with which to investigate the environmental, social and lifestyle causes of disease. They could also propose responses to public health problems that are not narrowly clinical, but that address the social problems that contribute to ill health. Physicians would, quite rightly, engage in matters of social policy since public health relates intricately with the institutional arrangements within which we make our lives – the links between licensing laws, social opportunity and the use of legal and illegal drugs could be explored with greater empirical zest.

More generally, academic researchers in the social as well as the physical sciences could use the money to support inquiry that serves the general interest, even when uninhibited inquiry poses problems for powerful private actors. Demography, development economics, and other playgrounds of the defence-intelligence imagination, could be opened up to lines of inquiry that do not assume a future of steepening inequality and permanent low-level conflict. Social scientists could provide the public with data that supports moves to use our vast productive capacity to secure the social forms we want. Engineers could seek support for work in developing alternatives to fossil fuels without needing to resort to an Anglo-American state apparatus that is at best ambivalent or to a private sector where the oil and gas companies retain overwhelming market power. As the general population takes direct control of more funds, it can use basic research into social and physical reality as the basis for investments in new technologies and new experiments in living. Social and economic organization should, after all, be determined in the light of publicly mandated research.

Researchers could also use the money to police the claims of scientists in the state and corporate sector and to establish the facts behind attempts by interested parties to manipulate the climate of opinion. Scientists have always been vulnerable when their work threatens to disrupt the existing pattern of power relations. Once the population fully grasps the emancipatory potential of free inquiry, it will perhaps work harder to ensure that scientists are not bullied or traduced when they try to speak out honestly. The scientific establishment remains riddled with unspoken taboos and political agendas. The pursuit of new knowledge constantly comes into conflict with the prerogatives of established power and varieties of self-interest.

At present we can only guess at the full extent to which states, corporations and other interests suppress research that threatens their prerogatives; in the absence of a parallel system of review our attitude depends on our personality. The sanguine are sanguine, the suspicious are suspicious. More profoundly, we do not know what potentially fruitful lines of inquiry are being starved of support in the current system. Public patronage of science will take us into the realm of fact. The distorting effects of private power on truth will be revealed, as part of a process by which resources are distributed in ways that address public concerns. One thing is certain. The public cannot be any worse at spending at least some of its own money than those who are currently responsible.

With a budget of only a few billion a year, an engaged public could come to understand much more clearly the causes of ill health and social distress and the responses to them that work. Researchers and scientists would be able to look to a source of funding that is beholden neither to the central state nor to profit-seeking institutions. This new system of public knowledge would make it possible for future policy decisions to take place in an environment that is not leached of information troublesome to the existing order. New forms of expertise would develop along with new means of accrediting experts. Knowledge generated with public funds would be connected to wider audiences through the same institutions that publicize the findings of publicly commissioned journalism. Journalists and scientists would collaborate to publicize their work, and to present proposals for change in the world.

Participation in decisions about the dispersal of funds for scientific research into public health would in itself go a considerable way to promoting sociability through collective endeavour. We are increasingly lonely, distracted or medicated and we lack the means to understand and to change our predicament. The sociability required if we are to develop an autonomous understanding of the world will itself bring important benefits. We already know that political participation of a meaningful kind itself constitutes an effective public health intervention.[26] If science is to serve the general good then we must participate to the full extent possible in the debate about the ends to which it is directed. This does not require untutored meddling in the details of the scientific method, only a proper concern for the objectives of science.

The significance of this reform of science can hardly be exaggerated. A parallel system of science would serve as a useful source of information about our own and other societies and about the physical world. It would provide oversight of the state and of the private interests with which science is currently intertwined. It would protect individual scientists and help the profession as a whole to align the stories it tells about science to the role that science plays in society.

It costs considerable sums to estrange scientists from the population at large and to establish the governing assumptions of science as it is currently structured. In a system of public science relatively small sums could challenge and change these assumptions and ensure that the pursuit of knowledge is made consonant with the common good.

In time, the public should participate directly in the decisions on research and development to the greatest possible extent. A system of transparent democratic commissioning that controls around 2 per cent of GDP would be sufficient to establish effective control of the scientific and technological legacy we leave our children. In creating and running such a system we would come to exercise substantial influence on 'the whole thrust of the economy'. Scientists would have greater freedom to explore society and nature and as patrons of science citizens would come to exercise effective control over the conditions in which they live. An openly discussed model of the future we want would inform the pursuit of knowledge. Though we are surrounded with rhetoric about democracy and freedom we currently struggle to make sense of a present that we had no hand in creating. Under conditions of formal freedom we experience life as a series of fresh defeats. This will not change until we develop a publicly accountable system for commissioning and then publicizing the operations of science. The reform of journalism and of science will change the constitution of knowledge in ways that will allow the populations of Britain and the United States to establish themselves as informed and, therefore, competent publics.

CHAPTER TWELVE

Reforming the Private Sector

T HE PREVIOUS TWO chapters have sketched a plan for reforming the constitution of knowledge. I have argued that the general population should have the power to commission both journalists and scientists to investigate matters of common concern. Sometimes this system will support lines of inquiry that seem frivolous or pernicious, but all of the claims and descriptions produced will be available for open debate. Public commissioning has the virtue of allowing individual citizens to have some degree of control over the distribution of professional curiosity. It therefore has the potential to replace what passes for public opinion with a clarified body of publicly accessible knowledge. The existing institutions that together inform the population will be subject to challenge by experts working directly for fractions of that population. Communication ceases to be something that one group does to another and becomes part of a process of mutual transformation through argument. As Christopher Lasch has noted: 'when we get into arguments that focus and fully engage our attention, we become avid seekers of relevant information'.[1] Much of the current economy of knowledge resembles an experiment in what will happen in the absence of such arguments. In a system of public commissioning, assumptions that are implicit in our social arrangements, and that the media often decline to discuss, become accessible to debate. New knowledge fuels new controversy. As we establish our opinions through debate and the exercise of commissioning power, we break from the silent, if restive, ranks of an audience and become members of a public.

I am not sure what we might make of this new, properly public, status. Certainly, the process of establishing a public regime of truth is bound to be chaotic. Resentments and frustrations created by the existing media – impatience with liberal bias and political correctness as well as concerns about 'corporate influence' and state manipulation, certain forms of political theology in which the forces of light contend with dark principalities and powers – will all have a chance to work their way through the commissioning process. Suspicions that largely go unacknowledged in the current institutions will secure some kind of investigative expression. Those who believe that something about the war on terror does not make sense will have a chance to hire investigators and publicize the information they bring to light. The radical left and the radical right will have a chance to make themselves more persuasive by seeking facts that support their ideas. Anti-Semites and Islamophobes will do what they can to share their version of the truth with the wider world. Public commissioning does not establish in advance the limits of acceptable description and so the early stages in particular will have their share of lunacy as well as breakthroughs. Still, in so far as public matters are concerned, I agree with Jefferson that 'there is not a truth existing which I fear, or would wish unknown to the whole world'.[2] Whatever is true, no matter how unlikely or unpleasant, deserves to be considered. Whatever is false, no matter how pleasing or plausible, deserves to be challenged in open debate. The products of prejudice and dishonesty will be destroyed by the same system that at times gives them form.

We cannot be certain about much beyond this initial period of confusion, but a properly public media system would perhaps allow us to establish the full impact of the neoliberal turn and to decide on a programme of remedies. Over the previous generation much has been made of the need to reform the public sector. For the most part this has meant selling state-owned properties to private business, importing market mechanisms into the civil service, removing regulations to encourage economic growth, and opening up public services to private contractors. The combined effect of these moves has been to transform government into a gigantic profit centre. Management consultants, IT companies, prison builders and operators, and the nightmare factory of homeland security have joined military contractors in a raid on tax revenues. In the United States the free-for-all has been noisy enough to stir the normally drowsy *New York Times* into remarking that 'without a public debate or formal policy decision, contractors have become a virtual fourth branch of government'.[3]

The financial crisis has shown that neoliberal reform of the public sector has left the state unable to protect the general interest. Rather than continuing under cover of the word reform to make the state more business-friendly, and hence more willing to transfer tax revenues to private interests, public commissioning would enable us to begin a much-needed reform of the private sector. Central to this reform is a transformation of the dominant institution of the private economy, the large corporation. Reform of the enterprise does no more than register what is now obvious; corporations dominate the production and distribution of physical, financial and intellectual capital to the point where the old image of individual competition in anarchic markets has become an irrelevance at best, at worst a kind of enchantment. State-like bureaucracies integrate ever more closely with the institutions of government and capture an ever larger share of both tax revenues and private income.

The enterprise in its current form does nothing to prepare the individual for active citizenship. The modern corporation trains up a few as courtiers and steeps the rest of us in a perpetual indignity. Its claims to inclusivity and its efforts to project a socially responsible image run directly contrary to its legal structure as a vehicle for maximizing shareholder value and to the interests of senior managers, who rightly see in an engaged workforce a threat to their own exalted positions. Power is opaque and arbitrary while greed and selfishness co-exist with deep irrationality.

For just as corporations reach out to the state and seek to transform it in their interests, they engage ever more intimately with their workforce, treating it as an object of both surveillance and manipulation. Employees are urged to think positive and as jobs become less secure the penalties for having the wrong attitude become ever more serious. As personality becomes central to progress in a space characterized by arbitrary power, the individual is driven to adopt regimes of self-auditing and self-exploitation in an effort to survive.[4] Executives and would-be executives marinade themselves in the works of Lao Tzu and Machiavelli while demanding that employees become better team players. Working relationships become superficial and paranoid as competition intensifies. The drive for short-term profits that enrich managers and their partners in the financial sector often encourages them to act in ways that damage the wider society and that undermine the long-term interests of the institution and its owners. In a touch that Orwell would have relished, managers justify their hollowing out of the companies they control through appeals to the notion of shareholder value. Meanwhile the current system of ownership gives managers the resources they need to shape the legislative process and the general constitution of ideas and descriptions. It was corporations that funded the massive propaganda campaign for neoliberal ideas in the late 1970s and that continue to pay for the public relations product that saturates journalism.

If a clarified system of public knowledge is to survive, the enterprise must be reformed. A properly democratic culture can hardly flourish if our workplaces are run as tyrannies. This reform of the enterprise need imply no infringement of the rights of private property. At present the shareholders of limited-liability corporations enjoy an important advantage over other private sector actors in that they are only liable for the mistakes and crimes of the entity they own to the sum of the capital they invest. The privilege of limited liability extends far beyond anything demanded by the classical champions of private property. A man who causes harm in the course of his work can be sued for the full cost of that harm to the point of personal ruin. A man who owns shares in a company that causes the same harm risks only his original investment. The privilege of limited liability is justified on the grounds that it promotes economic dynamism; by limiting their risk the corporate form encourages investors to support innovative companies.

The major banks, structured to take advantage of limited liability, have lost vast sums and only state support has saved them. Though many shareholders have lost some or all of their original investment they are not liable for damage caused by the companies they owned. Meanwhile the general population stands squarely behind the massive debts incurred to save the global economy from collapse. It seems reasonable to conclude, as Berle and Means did after the Wall Street Crash, that owners who are not fully responsible for the actions of the corporation have 'surrendered the right that the corporation be operated in their sole interest' and that, since the actions of private companies can have wide-ranging public consequences, the public 'is in a position to demand that the modern corporation serve not alone the owners or the control but all society'.[5]

Limited liability in its current form has not delivered the general benefits that were claimed for it; as such, there can be no principled objections to reforms that inculcate a proper prudence into the actions of large commercial concerns. I propose that limited liability be reserved for those companies whose employees have a controlling interest in management, either as cooperatives or as employee-owned corporations where each employee has an equal share in the controlling trust. In this way workers can deliberate on matters that concern them as both citizens and employees. If, as Walter Rathenau suggested, the business enterprise has come to resemble the state in character, it is high time that republican democracy shaped both its actions in the world and its internal culture.

Employees are more concerned with the long-term viability of the company than with its short-term profitability. It is likely that they will prevent managers from behaving in ways that jeopardize their own livelihoods. Asset stripping, ill-considered mergers and takeovers, and financial engineering will all become less attractive in companies where the overriding preoccupation is with maintaining stable and rewarding conditions of employment. This move to restrict the benefits of limited liability would not mean expropriating the current owners of large commercial enterprises. Quite minor changes in the law governing limited liability could ensure that market forces changed patterns of ownership and control in favour of workers and pensioners. Private companies could continue to enjoy limited liability, the better to encourage entrepreneurial initiative. Again, the tax law could be changed to encourage the sale of these companies to their employees as owner-founders die or seek to realize the value of their equity. If the capitalist is to survive as a specific social type he or she should be made to focus on bringing new products to the open market rather than on speculative activity and accumulation through fraud.

Under a properly constituted system of employee ownership, the enterprise ceases to be so thoroughly toxic to the human beings whose actions give it substance. Instead of providing funds with which owners and senior managers can intimidate their employees and dominate the political process, enterprises instead become schools for deliberation on matters of general concern. Instead of acting as a barrier between the working majority and the world of legislation and administration, the enterprise becomes a natural point of contact with that world. Employees can debate how surpluses are spent and will have an opportunity to use money that they have, after all, earned, to defend and promote their collective interests. The sums currently spent by corporations on political communications could be used to fund political movements that protect the rights of working people. Employee-owned corporations could also support moves to establish national and international regulatory regimes that limit exploitation and ensure that the benefits of increasing productivity are distributed fairly.

This is not to be naïve. The markets in which companies operate will remain competitive. Indeed, as state-funded research becomes more widely available, new technology will quicken competition by removing the advantages currently enjoyed by favoured sectors. Power relationships will persist within the enterprise; the interests of managers and workers will continue to clash. Something like the separation of powers that political theorists of the eighteenth century described will be needed to prevent managers from translating their information advantages into illicit profits. Trade unions will continue to play a role, therefore, both as advisors to the workforce in their dealings with management, and as advisors to individual enterprises in their dealings with one another and with the state. The tension between the desires for justice and for individual advantage will persist.

Given that the beneficial owners of employee-controlled companies will also be taxpayers in countries where the companies are based, there will be fewer incentives to engage in tax-avoidance. Much of what we think of as international trade takes place within large companies; in the current system this frees up vast sums for insiders to use to enrich themselves and corrupt others. The profits generated by employee-owned companies that are not needed for reinvestment will find their way back to employees and can be properly taxed. Furthermore, there will also be less enthusiasm for contracting out production offshore and companies will work harder to respond to competition and technological changes in ways that serve the interests of all employees.

A shift away from large corporations with external shareholders would have important consequences for the financial sector. Corporate debt generates huge profits for banks, as does speculation on the stock market. Financiers have been able to persuade the directors of large companies to engage in aggressive expansion schemes that increase levels of borrowing, with the implicit threat of a hostile takeover if they refuse to cooperate. Pension funds have repeatedly lost out in a game controlled by senior managers and investment bankers. In future, bankers will have to persuade a majority of employees that takeovers, sale and leaseback deals and other forms of financial engineering are in the long-term interests of the enterprise. The reduced scope for outside share ownership limits in turn the scope for financial speculation in shares. Many equity traders and analysts will have to find something else to do with their time. The more talented among them will perhaps find useful work in the trade unions.

There are persuasive arguments for wide-ranging reform of finance. Privately held banks have yet again proved unequal to the task of providing credit in a responsible way. The recent chaos in the financial markets and the wider economy is only the latest expression of the financial sector's tendency to serve its own short-term interests at everyone's long-term expense. Banking remains mysterious to most people and bankers have tried hard to keep it that way. The situation now is hardly different from that of the early 1970s when the government removed controls on lending on the basis of 'a gentleman's agreement in private conclaves in the City'.[6] Money and close links with the institutions of the state have allowed finance to manipulate the political process and the economy of ideas to the point where Wall Street and the City define the limits of the possible in their respective countries. Public commissioning combined with a reformed pattern of ownership in the economy will provide the means to break their hold on Anglo-America.

At present too few of us understand the financial system well enough to know how to reform it, even though, as J. K. Galbraith once remarked, 'the process by which the banks create money is so simple, the mind is repelled'.[7] But after the events of the last few years all of us can appreciate that the creation of credit is fraught with the potential for abuse. And even a brief examination of the historical record shows that privately owned banks have repeatedly jeopardized the common wealth by exploiting the arcane power of debt creation. Finance should be subject to a prolonged inquiry by the population organized as publics, to determine whether and how it should be reformed. Perhaps they will conclude that the central banks in Britain and the United States should only loan money to publicly accountable institutions. State-owned development banks could fund industrial expansion in particular regions and sectors and defined publics would exercise responsible control over their activities. Private banks could continue to take deposits from private savers and use them to make loans. But they would no longer have access to the state's capacity to generate near limitless credit. They would have less power to create bubbles in asset markets; and they would no longer need to be bailed out by taxpayers who do not understand and are required simply to believe, the fate of the sucker through the ages.

Of course a public system of credit might lead to reckless cronyism or bureaucratic torpor. But the current system already does. Employee-owned companies might become unjust and sclerotic. But the corporations they would replace already are. Once generally distributed knowledge provides the basis for legislation, the people might still decide that the current structure of the private sector cannot be improved without unacceptable risks. Or they might decide to abolish private property and try to create a world without exploitation. My own hope is that they will move steadily to democratize the workplace and the system of credit in the context of a shift from private luxury to public justice.

But whatever we think might emerge from open deliberation, we can only expect changes to be both durable and successful if they are widely understood and strongly supported by an informed population. If together we find that our current arrangements, after steady examination, cannot be defended, then together we must devise their replacement. As we discover the world through argument and debate we may begin to trace the outlines of the world we want. A republican system of communications, in which we are both able and motivated to understand, is a necessary condition for democratic government.

CONCLUSION:

A Commonwealth of Descriptions

We are what we repeatedly do. Excellence is not an act, but a habit.

Aristotle

IN THE SEVENTEENTH century, English opponents of absolute monarchy rediscovered the classical notion of a public of citizens. This public, they argued, should function as the sovereign power in the state.[1] While at times they suggested that public sovereignty would strengthen the state, their key argument for a Republic revolved around their understanding of liberty. Rather than seeing liberty as a private possession, the English republicans saw it as a product, or by-product, of public exertion. Human flourishing – properly human identity – depends not merely on freedom from constraint, but on a shared freedom to determine the conditions of our shared life.

Later articulations of the idea of the public served to obscure the classically inspired notion that public status depended on the power to shape the actions of the state. Two traditions in particular have come to dominate our understanding of the word 'public' – or rather, it features in two highly influential ways of thinking about social organization. The first asserts that public-minded administrators – pre-eminently 'civil servants' – can identify and secure the common good. The Democratic Party in the United States, the Labour Party in Britain, as well as liberal Republicans and One Nation Tories accepted this notion between the Depression and the end of the 1970s. The second tradition, dominant after around 1980 in both Britain and the US, insists that individuals seeking to satisfy their preferences through market exchange will secure the general interest to the greatest possible extent, so long as they are left alone by the state. Public benefits, it is claimed, can best be secured by private means.

Though these two traditions sometimes seem to exhaust the possibilities of controversy – glossed with reference to Keynes and Friedman they more or less cover the spectrum of admissible thought in economics, for example – they both stand opposed to the republican notion that the common good can only be established and preserved by the collective actions of a body of free citizens. Both the public service ethos and neoliberalism seek to do without a population operating as an autonomous public. In the first, well-meaning technocrats, who are properly responsive to the reasonable demands of the population, deliver the best of all possible worlds. In the second, market forces are left to do the work.

Part 2 of this book offered a summary of what three decades of reliance on market forces has done to the economy of knowledge in Anglo-America.[2] Neoliberalism has clearly failed to provide citizens with an accurate account of the world. I have only been able to sketch some of the key failures of the modern media and to give some suggestions as to why the mainstream press, as seems undeniable, cannot state the facts plainly and consistently according to a rationally justifiable scale of priorities.

The eclipse of the public as a source of decision-making seems to be reflected in the language and the preoccupations of the modern media. The British and American media's insistence on their right to publish the private affairs of individuals 'in the public interest' undermines the practice of constitutional politics. If one denies those who aspire to public status the right to a private life one effectively grants veto power to those who can assemble the facts of our ordinary existence. As animals driven by the necessity of self-love we are all at times faithless, duplicitous, cruel; or delusional or ridiculous or mentally unstable. If we limit public life to those who are privately blameless we will be able to choose our politicians from a tiny handful of people who are less than human; or else from those who have brokered deals with the institutions that govern publicity. The rest of us will stand in permanent danger of exposure as . . . human beings. For who among us is not, at a sufficient degree of magnification, disgusting? The right to a private life secures the possibility of public existence. Without it all public figures are subject to the same implicit blackmail. To treat what is private as public, just as to treat what is public as private, amounts to a kind of tyranny.

The term public relations points to the same eclipse. From its origins in the 1920s modern public relations has sought to prevent the population from establishing itself as an autonomous body of informed citizens who communicate effectively amongst themselves and respond effectively to claims made by powerful individuals and interests. The public relations industry sets itself the task of forestalling and frustrating the public in the interests of its clients, and in this it builds on the work of earlier pioneers in manipulating the press. The subordination of the mass media to private or sectional interests long pre-dates the careers of Lippmann and Bernays, especially in the consequential realms of war and economic organization. J. A. Hobson argued at the beginning of the twentieth century that 'a small body of men' had secured popular support for an aggressive war in South Africa 'by the simple device of securing all important avenues of intelligence, and of using them to inject into the public mind a continuous stream of false and distorted information'.[3] The same tricks have played out repeatedly in the decades that followed. The blurring of political propaganda and commercial promotion, the appeals to patriotic zeal and humanitarian sentiment, and the steady desire of a restless few to secure their interests by force and fraud would not have surprised Hobson.

The post-war era certainly saw a number of triumphs for well-funded and well-staffed newsrooms. But at the same time the institutions of the state thoroughly insinuated themselves into the operations of civil society. As a result the organizing assumptions of British and American society remained outside the terms of widely publicized debate. The increasing reliance of newspapers on material generated by public relations companies has been noted by a number of critics.[4] Journalism has been deskilled and journalists have been subjected to work rates that make even elementary fact-checking difficult and render long-term investigations all but impossible. But while the failings of journalism in the neoliberal era are glaringly obvious, the remedy is not to be found in the practices and assumptions of the years between the Second World War and 1980.

In the final section of the book I outlined a programme of media reform that addresses the connected problems of state propaganda and the efforts of the rich to distort the field of publicity. I argued that those who wish to research should be able to appeal directly to the population who will constitute their audience. The population must act as the unmediated patron of journalists and investigators, to the extent that it wishes to do so, if it is to retain the power to reshape general understanding in light of the observable facts. Given the size of the consequential institutions and the distance between the majority and the points of decision, it is only when a population achieves autonomy in this sense that it becomes a public.

In practical terms this raises obvious problems. The population would benefit from securing a public status for itself. Journalists would benefit, too, from a funding model that ties a successful career more firmly and transparently to the approval of at least some fraction of the audience. But the institutions that currently govern the content of widely shared communications have less to gain. Neither public service broadcasters nor the employees of large private media conglomerates can be expected to welcome an approach that takes for granted that they have collectively failed to perform the task they claimed for themselves. Still, I offer the idea of public commissioning to those who are serious about constitutional change in the widest sense. Knowledge is power and changes to the constitution of knowledge must in turn affect the constitution of power. The coming years will see the need for very rapid change if we are to fend off environmental collapse, economic crisis and the awful adventure of war without end. Rapid change of the sort needed will only be possible if the distribution of knowledge can be made to serve the interests of the population as a whole rather than the privileges of small groups of men. If nothing else, public commissioning offers us the prospect of rejecting and reversing the upwards transfer of wealth from the working majority to the minority of owners and investors. Calls for fiscal discipline and for restraints on all the many tricks of accumulation by fraud can only be answered by a public system of inquiry and communication.

Writing in the mid-1970s Richard Sennett worried that the habit of cooperation with strangers in pursuit of shared goals had steadily given way to a 'culture of authenticity', in which the openly dramatic performance of public life was replaced by the artifice of the seemingly authentic candidate. Sennett noted how his contemporaries had come to value candour and informality; people looked to the person rather than the programme and found the mannered distance of the statesman distasteful – 'public man' had lost ground to politicians who sought to establish a private rapport.[5] The trouble that Sennett identified has been a feature of elections ever since. The candidate best able to produce a simulacrum of unaffected affability enjoys an often-decisive advantage. In this way the content of public life has been hollowed out and politics has become the exclusive preserve of more or less humane supporters of an insupportable status quo.[6]

The field of publicity has filled up with the billboard-sized intimacies of celebrity and corporate communications; brands and human beings re-imagined and refined by the entertainment industry combine and compete for our attention and affection. The state and commercial institutions alike seek to shape private and intimate arrangements; the construction of character becomes a means of persuasion.[7] The practice of public commissioning would allow us to learn how to engage with one another as public actors, and to populate this field of publicity according to openly debated assessments of what is required. The process of public commissioning, with its mixture of formal and informal meetings and its equality of commissioning power, offers us an education in the kind of public life that Sennett feared was vanishing from the modern world. Through regular commissioning of inquiry and through the management of publicity we would learn how to live as free citizens. Furthermore, public commissioning provides us with the means to challenge the forms of social of disparagement that press in on us under conditions of steepening inequality and insecurity. Since the work of public commissioning feeds directly into the common stock of descriptions it will enable us to challenge those stories that intimidate and diminish us. To the extent that these stories are factually flawed, it will allow us to destroy them. Public commissioning thus provides us with both the means to assert ourselves publicly and the motives for doing so.

This is not to pretend that inequality won't remain, or that public commissioning won't need to be checked and challenged by other forms of newsgathering and investigation. Furthermore it would be a mistake to imagine that it won't be affected by the disparities of power and prestige that exist elsewhere. People become conditioned to believe that they are incapable of effective action, that achieving change is someone else's responsibility. To some extent public commissioning will belong to those who are already articulate and confident. But, by giving a simple power of command to all citizens, the mechanism offers us a taste of what it would be like to live in a world re-described. The many institutions that seek to promote participation and diversity could concentrate on giving those who lack experience and confidence a training in spoken and written rhetoric, thereby allowing individuals and groups to assert themselves in public without the need for community leaders or well-meaning professionals to articulate their concerns for them.

At present, as Pierre Bourdieu noted, 'the game is rigged in favour of the professionals of speech, of authorized speech'. To establish a truer equality, 'we would need to favour the disfavoured (help them with gestures and looks, give them time, etc.). Whereas everything is done to favour the favoured.'[8] The original division of the private world of the household and the public world of political action was accompanied by a denigration of women and children and an anxious insistence on the exclusive right of a minority of men to determine the substance of policy. The sites of effective decision remain a playground for a certain kind of middle-aged male. If public institutions of the sort I propose are to flourish they must extend participation to those who were once explicitly denied a public status and who are now effectively marginalized – women above all.

The mass media have always relied on state intervention and subsidy even if the beneficiaries of the current system have tended to avoid discussion of this fact. But a debate about the future of the media will have to take place, since, as McChesney and Nichols point out, 'the business that sustained commercial news media for the past century is dying'.[9] Maintaining a national system of knowledge will require that subsidies be expanded in one way or another; state involvement in the media is, and always has been, inevitable. The question is how this involvement is organized. Technocratic managers and private owners, not to mention the coordinating forces of the state, will all prefer that the discussion of media reform remains limited to a debate between neoliberals and public servants. Public commissioning offers journalists, academics and reformers the means to widen this debate by appealing to the interests of the general population.

Public commissioning, then, rejects both neoliberalism and the public service ethic as adequate bases for social organization, initially in the field of publicity. But the implications of this rejection reach far further into the organization of professional and scientific knowledge and finally into the systems of economic and political power. By giving the population a share in the construction of opinion, public commissioning gives substance to the notion that government rests on popular consent. Able to inform itself on the issues it deems relevant, the citizen body could finally subject the governing assumptions of British and American society to effective scrutiny.

Most of us have been living with an inadequate account of the world for the last 30 years. While it is possible to assemble the outlines of an alternative account that is better grounded in the facts, it remains difficult, if not impossible, to share that alternative with others. Even if we have the time and resources to test and revise the claims and descriptions that most people are exposed to, mediating institutions retain an effectual monopoly on decisions that affect the general field of publicity. We have few incentives for unencumbered investigation, especially since our efforts are likely to set us at odds with the main currents of opinion. No one wants to be seen as a crank or a conspiracy theorist, or to subject themselves to condescension or contempt from those who are given ample licence to speak authoritatively and whose claims can rarely be challenged in open debate.

The current arrangement of power broadly defined has left us unable to articulate ourselves as an autonomous and finally sovereign public. The media reform I propose allows us to remedy this by making generally available the means and the motive to learn about each other and the world. From a revised body of shared descriptions we can hope to assemble a new set of opinions about the legitimacy of our current arrangements.

This change in the general climate of opinion will have unpredictable effects on the course of our shared life. I have suggested how it might lead to changes in the economy and in the structure of decision-making that reach far beyond media reform as such. I might be wrong in detail and in general. But we do not know. Some fairly minor changes in the structure of media provision would offer us the chance to find out. We should ask ourselves whether it is time to establish a new model of reporting, one that promises to generate a commonwealth of descriptions – a necessary, if not sufficient, resource in the work of making another world possible. A group of people capable of changing their opinions in light of information they have themselves commissioned can claim to be free. A society organized in this way can claim to be in a substantive sense enlightened. If we come to organize the distribution of journalistic and scientific curiosity in the way I have outlined, then we will have reassembled as a public – for the first time perhaps as a universal public.

Acknowledgements

IN THIS BOOK I have covered a good deal of ground that was unknown to me when I started and it seems right that I make formal note of my very considerable debts. If I have been able to offer readers anything new, it is only because I have made so free a use of the work of others. On the nature of republican thought I have relied heavily on Quentin Skinner's work, especially his *Liberty Before Liberalism*. The late Roy Porter's *Enlightenment: Britain and the Creation of the Modern World* was an invaluable source for contemporary attitudes to power and the role of the public in eighteenth-century Britain. On the development of the United States I have borrowed heavily from the work of C. Wright Mills. I also found Stuart Ewen's *PR! A Social History of Spin* and Christopher Simpson's *Science of Coercion* exceptionally useful.

My sense of how recent developments have impacted on the individual has been formed in part by Barbara Ehrenreich's books. My remarks on the structure of the enterprise owe a considerable amount to the Larry Elliott and Dan Atkinson's *The Gods That Failed* and to David Erdal's writings on industrial democracy. Nick Shaxson's forthcoming book on offshore finance has confirmed the sense that an adequate account of political economy – indeed a tolerably accurate description of reality – must take secrecy jurisdictions into account.

The discussion of Lippmann in Chapter 4 and the account of the gap between popular attitudes and those of the elite given in Chapter 8 in particular draw heavily on Noam Chomsky's political writings. The discussion of science, technology and industrial production in

Chapter 11 also owes him a considerable debt. The use I have made of these ideas is, of course, my own responsibility.

I have benefited from conversations and advice from many quarters in the writing of the book. Jörg Hengsen, Canan Gündüz, Greg Muttitt, Hannah Robson, Philip Augar, and Jake Osborne asked exactly the right awkward questions, encouraged new lines of thought, and talked me out of at least some errors. Thank you. Anna Minton read the material on public commissioning and suggested some very useful improvements. I am profoundly grateful to my friend Stefanie Marsh. I am not sure I could have finished the book without you. My parents, Diana and Geoffrey Hind, have always encouraged and supported me in my work and this last year would have been much harder to endure had it not been for you. Perry Walker and Stephen Whitehead at the New Economics Foundation provided a welcome forum to test ideas. Tamasin Cave at Spinwatch has proved that the public interest need not always lose out to private power. I'd also like to thank the staff at the British Library, a great public institution.

At Verso, Sarah Shin and Rowan Wilson have been tremendously good fun to work with and have showed exemplary patience towards an author who is keenly aware of how irritating authors can be and who still can't help himself. My copy-editor, Tim Clark, worked hard to save me from all manner of pratfalls. Needless to say, those that remain are my own. Mark Martin presided over the final production of the text with remarkable patience.

Tom Penn commissioned the book and, as with *The Threat to Reason*, showed me how it might be made to resemble more closely the book I had in mind. Thank you for your advice and encouragement. I hope that the preceding does justice to your confidence in me. Thanks too to Andrew Kidd at Aitken Alexander, for your reassuring good sense.

This book must serve as a substitute for the book I lacked the skill to write. It is also, necessarily, at least as much a product of selfish discontent as of magnanimous disinterest. I can only hope that the ordinary tangle of private motives that led me to think about the public has led me to create something that proves of general benefit, and that what I was unable to say, to one person in particular, becomes instead some good in the world.

London, July 2010

Notes

1 Introduction

1 In the words of the Nobel Prize–winning economist Joseph Stiglitz, 'Most of the individual mistakes [that led to the financial crisis] boil down to just one: a belief that markets are self-adjusting and that the role of the government should be minimal'. Joseph Stiglitz, 'Capitalist Fools', *Vanity Fair*, January 2009.

2 Edmund L. Andrews, 'Greenspan Concedes Error on Regulation', *New York Times*, 23 October 2008.

3 Andrew Clark, Jill Treanor, 'Greenspan – I Was Wrong About the Economy. Sort Of', *Guardian*, 24 October 2008.

4 Michael Sandel, 'A New Politics of the Common Good', Reith Lecture 4, BBC Radio 4, 30 June 2009.

5 Quoted in James Curran and Jean Seaton, *Power Without Responsibility* (London: Routledge, 2003), p. 393.

6 Sean O'Grady, 'Summers Cautions on Modest US Recovery', *Independent*, 1 February 2010.

7 Stephen Foley, 'Paulson and Bernanke Savaged over Bailout Plan', *Independent*, 24 September 2008.

8 Edmund L. Andrews, 'Wave of Debt Payments Facing U.S. Government', *New York Times*, 22 November 2009; Gràinne Gilmore, 'Public Debt Soars to Record at 61.7% of GDP', *The Times*, 22 January 2010.

9 David Marquand, *The Decline of the Public* (Cambridge: Polity, 2004); Jürgen Habermas, *The Structural Transformation of the Public Sphere* (Cambridge: Polity, 1989).

10 *Oxford English Dictionary* (Oxford: Oxford University Press, 2001), pp. 778–86

11 See Ha-Joon Chang, *Kicking Away the Ladder* (Anthem: London, 2002) for an account of how countries have industrialized and then made up stories about the process for foreign and domestic consumption. See also Robert C. Allen, *Enclosure and the Yeoman* (Oxford: Oxford University Press, 1992) for a challenge to the widely promoted notion that economic development requires steeper inequality.

12 See Frances Stonor Saunders, *Who Paid the Piper? The CIA and the Cultural Cold War* (London: Granta, 1999), Lori Lyn Boyle, *The Pentagon's Battle for the American Mind* (College Station: Texas A&M University Press, 2004) and Richard Sennett, *The Fall of Public Man* (London: Faber, 1993) for an introduction to the ways in which the operations and habits of private and public life have become scrambled.

1 The Classical Public

1 Valerius Maximus, *Memorable Doings and Sayings*, Book II, 2.4b.

2 Habermas, *The Structural Transformation of the Public Sphere*, p. 11.

3 Martin Dzelzainis, 'Milton's Classical Republicanism', in David Armitage, Quentin Skinner and Armand Himy (eds.), *Milton and Republicanism* (Cambridge: Cambridge University Press, 1995), pp. 3–7. Spelling revised.

4 Quoted from the official website of the British monarchy: www.royal.gov.uk

5 Quoted in Quentin Skinner, 'Rethinking Political Liberty', *History Workshop Journal*, 61, Spring 2006, pp. 156–70.

6 James Harrington, *The Commonwealth of Oceana* (London: Routledge, 1887), p. 178.

7 Quoted in Quentin Skinner, *Liberty Before Liberalism* (Cambridge: Cambridge University Press, 1998), p. 71.

8 Sallust, *Bellum Catilinae*, 20.7, author's translation.

9 The aristocracy feared monarchy for this reason. The Republic gave each of them the chance to enjoy the magnificence of monarchial power within limits set by the constitution.

10   Michael J. Braddick, 'Civility and Authority', in David Armitage and Michael J. Braddick (eds.), *The British Atlantic World, 1500–1800* (Houndmills: Palgrave, 2009), p. 114.

11   Jonathan Scott, *Commonwealth Principles* (Cambridge: Cambridge University Press, 2004), p. 157.

12   Victoria Kahn, 'The Metaphorical Contract', in Armitage et al. (eds.), *Milton and Republicanism*, p. 88.

13   Harrington, *The Commonwealth of Oceana*, p. 18.

14   Ibid., p. 9.

15   Ibid., p. 61.

16   Ibid., p. 39–40.

17   Algernon Sidney, quoted in Skinner, *Liberty Before Liberalism*, p. 93.

18   C. Wright Mills, *The Power Elite* (New York: Oxford, 2000), p. 11.

19   Quoted in *Liberty Before Liberalism*, p. 78.

20   Thomas Hobbes, *Leviathan* (Oxford: Oxford University Press, 2008), p. 141.

21   Harrington, *The Commonwealth of Oceana*, pp. 26–7.

22   Ibid., p. 27.

23   Isaiah Berlin, *The Proper Study of Mankind* (London: Pimlico, 1998), p. 196.

24   Ibid., p. 203.

25   Ibid., p. 237.

26   Christopher Hill (ed.), *Winstanley: The Law of Freedom and Other Writings* (Cambridge: Cambridge University Press, 2006) p. 294.

27   Ibid., p. 295.

28   Bill of Rights, available online at http://avalon.law.yale.edu

2   Private Vices and Public Virtues

1   David Hume, 'Of the Protestant Succession', in *Selected Essays* (Oxford: Oxford University Press, 2008), p. 294.

2   *The Letters of Edward Gibbon*, ed. J. E. Norton (Cassell: London, 1956), vol. 2, p. 243.

3 Roy Porter, *Enlightenment: Britain and the Creation of the Modern World* (London: Penguin, 2001), p. 54.

4 Ibid., p. 39.

5 Quoted in Kees van der Pijl, *Transnational Classes and International Relations* (London: Routledge, 1998), p. 71.

6 See Richard Altick, *The English Common Reader* (Chicago: Chicago University Press, 1963).

7 Ben Wilson, *What Price Liberty?* (London: Faber and Faber, 2009), p. 34.

8 The phrase comes from 'The Dispensary', a poem by Sir Samuel Garth.

9 An official proclamation quoted in Habermas, *The Structural Transformation*, p. 59. Spelling amended.

10 Oliver Goldsmith quoted in Porter, *Enlightenment*, p. 94.

11 Habermas, *The Structural Transformation*, p. 42.

12 Quoted in ibid., p. 65–6.

13 Ibid., p. 64.

14 Henry Fielding, *Tom Jones* (Harmondsworth: Penguin, 1985), p. 272.

15 Michael J. Hogan, *A Cross of Iron* (Cambridge: Cambridge University Press, 1998), p. 419. Similar definitions could be found in many places.

16 Edmund B. Lambeth, 'Public Journalism as Democratic Practice', in Edmund B. Lambeth, Philip E. Meyer and Esther Thorson (eds.), *Assessing Public Journalism* (Columbia: University of Missouri Press, 1998), p. 21.

17 Michael Schudson, 'What Public Journalism Knows about Journalism but Doesn't Know about Public', in Theodore L. Glasser (ed.), *The Idea of Public Journalism* (New York: Guilford, 1999), pp. 122–3.

18 For a savage settling of accounts with 'public journalism', see Thomas Frank, *One Market Under God* (London: Random House, 2001). American enthusiasm for Habermas takes on an ironic edge when one notes the similarities between his work and that of C. Wright Mills. Habermas's distinction between *system* and *lifeworld*, for example, maps closely onto Mills' distinction between *structure* and *milieu*. Habermas quotes from Mills' description of the ideal type of

the public in the conclusion of *The Structural Transformation of the Public Sphere*, but American scholars have for the most part failed to note the influence on Habermas's thought of the great homegrown critic of American academic complacency – as far as I can tell from my far from comprehensive survey of the relevant work.

19   Quoted in Edmund S. Morgan, *Inventing the People: The Rise of Popular Sovereignty in England and America* (New York: W. W. Norton, 1988), pp. 220–1.

20   This is not to say that the population outside Parliament was entirely powerless or passive. The campaigns to end the slave trade and for constitutional reform both derived some of their force from popular movements.

21   J. C. D. Clark, *English Society, 1660–1832: Religion, Ideology and Politics During the Ancien Regime* (Cambridge: Cambridge University Press, 2000), p. 211.

22   Porter, *Enlightenment*, p. 392.

23   David Hume, 'Of Essay Writing', in *Selected Essays*, p. 1.

24   Quoted in Porter, *Enlightenment*, p. 54.

25   Quoted in Dorinda Outram, *The Enlightenment* (Cambridge: Cambridge University Press, 2005), p. 11. The passage appears in the 1769 draft of *The Wealth of Nations*, though not in later versions.

26   David Hume, 'Of the First Principles of Government', in *Selected Essays*, p. 24.

27   Ibid., p. 25.

28   James Boswell, *The Life of Samuel Johnson* (Harmondsworth: Penguin, 2008), p. 435.

29   Ellen Meiskins Wood, *Empire of Capital* (London: Verso, 2005).

30   Liberalism in this sense not only describes the world, it seeks to justify the private pursuit of profit in moral terms as the means by which the public interest is secured. Self-interest is thereby made an occasion for the most exquisite self-satisfaction.

31   Immanuel Kant, *An Answer to the Question: What is Enlightenment?* (London: Penguin, 2009), p. 1. Translation revised by the author.

32 Academics might seem to embody the enlightened ideal of disinterested, public reason. But, as we shall see, forces outside the university bear down on researchers in ways that have often effectively privatized their activities. Modern scholarship owes much to the Enlightenment, but it is not in some simple sense enlightened.

33 Quoted in Jonathan Israel, *Radical Enlightenment* (Cambridge: Harvard University Press, 2002), p. 719.

34 Porter, *Enlightenment*, p. 2.

3 Public Servants

1 Philip Harling, *The Waning of 'Old Corruption': The Politics of Economic Reform in Britain, 1779–1846*, (Oxford: Clarendon Press, 1996), p. 4. The role of Evangelical morality in driving this new public ideology does not feature prominently in contemporary discussions of the public sphere.

2 Robert Neild, *Public Corruption: The Dark Side of Social Evolution* (London: Anthem, 2002), p. 64.

3 Hannah Arendt, *The Human Condition* (Chicago: Chicago University Press, 1999), pp. 45–6.

4 Geoffrey Barraclough, *An Introduction to Contemporary History* (London: Penguin, 1990), p. 125

5 Quoted in David Marquand, *Decline of the Public: The Hollowing-out of Citizenship* (Cambridge: Polity, 2004), p. 37.

6 Benjamin Ginsberg, *The Captive Public: How Mass Opinion Promotes State Power* (New York: Basic Books, 1986), p. 34.

7 Quoted in Edward Bridges, *Portrait of a Profession: The Civil Service Tradition* (Cambridge: Cambridge University Press, 1950), pp. 14–15.

8 Benjamin Ginsberg, *The Captive Public: How Mass Opinion Promotes State Power* (New York: Basic Books, 1986), p. 29.

9 Robert Skidelsky, quoted in Curran and Seaton, *Power Without Responsibility*, pp. 114–15

10 Marquand, *Decline of the Public*, p. 27.

11 Bridges, *Portrait of a Profession*, p. 25.

12 Michael Sandel, 'Markets and Morals', Reith Lecture 1, BBC Radio 4, 13 June 2009.

13 Quoted in Seaton and Curran, *Power Without Responsibility*, p. 168.

14 Peter Hennessy, *Whitehall* (London: Fontana, 1990), p. 628.

15 Ibid.

16 Colin Leys, *Market-Driven Politics: Neoliberal Democracy and the Public Interest* (London: Verso, 2003), p. 216.

17 Joseph Schumpeter, quoted in Leo Panitch and Colin Leys, *The End of Parliamentary Socialism* (London: Verso, 1997), p. 11.

18 Bridges, *Portrait of a Profession*, pp. 27, 31.

19 The public service ethic, like liberalism in the capitalist mode, moralises the pursuit of self-interest. The public servants luxuriate in high-grade information and the exercise of their intellect while feeling sure that what they do is in the public interest, that it contributes to the common good.

4 The American Republic

1 Quoted in Clark, *English Society, 1660–1832*, p. 127.

2 Quoted in Kees van der Pijl, *Transnational Classes and International Relations*, p. 68.

3 Leslie Marchand (ed.), *Lord Byron: Selected Letters and Journals* (Cambridge, MA: Harvard University Press, 1982), p. 282.

4 Quoted in William Leach, *Land of Desire* (New York: Pantheon, 1993), p. 236.

5 Woodrow Wilson, *The New Freedom* (London: Chapman and Hall, 1913), p. 10.

6 Ibid., p. 9.

7 Adolf A. Berle and Gardiner C. Means, *The Modern Corporation and Private Property* (New York: Macmillan, 1933), p. 349.

8 Walter Lippmann, *Public Opinion* (New York: Simon and Schuster, 1997), p. 19.

9   Ibid., p. 171.

10   Ibid., p. 306. On 23 April 2010, the lead stories on Yahoo UK news included: 'What a Whopper, Mum's giant bundle of joy', 'Man finds sea lion on his roof' and 'Baseball star's "Superman" leap'.

11   Lippmann, *Public Opinion*, p. 55.

12   Ibid., p. 64.

13   Ibid., p. 49.

14   Ibid., p. 195.

15   Ibid., p. 230.

16   Ibid., p. 19.

17   Ibid., p. 246.

18   Ibid., p. 240.

19   Walter Lippmann, *The Phantom Public* (New York: Macmillan, 1925), p. 15. The point is echoed by one of the authors of NSM-68, the founding text of the Cold War.

20   Edward Bernays, *Propaganda* (New York: Ig Publishing, 1928), pp. 75–6.

21   Ibid., p. 127.

22   Ibid., p. 72.

23   Ibid., p. 73.

24   Ibid., p. 48.

25   Graham Wallas, *Human Nature in Politics* (London: Constable, 1908), p. 5.

26   Dewey, *The Public and Its Problems*, p. 219.

27   Ibid., p. 109.

28   Ibid., p. 31.

29   The right has been highly effective in mobilizing popular sentiment through appeals to the image of the nineteenth-century Republic of small towns.

30   William Peter Hamilton, quoted in Peter Krass, *The Book of Investing Wisdom* (New York: Wiley, 1999), p. 213.

31   Quoted in C. Wright Mills, *White Collar: The American Middle Classes* (New York: Oxford University Press, 2002), p. 145.

32 'Recommendations to the Congress to Curb Monopolies and the Concentration of Economic Power', 29 April 1938.

33 W. Lance Bennett and Jarol B. Manheim, *The Big Spin: Strategic Communication and the Transformation of Pluralist Democracy* in W. Lance Bennett and Robert M. Entman (eds.), *Mediated Politics* (Cambridge: Cambridge University Press, 2001), p. 279.

34 Robert Dahl, *Pluralist Democracy in the United States* (Chicago: Rand McNally, 1967), p. 24.

35 Ibid., p. 386.

36 Daniel Bell, *The End of Ideology* (Cambridge, MA: Harvard University Press, 2000), p. 402.

37 Quoted in Leonard Silk and David Vogel, *Ethics and Profits: The Crisis of Confidence in American Business* (New York: Simon and Schuster, 1976), p. 43.

38 Quoted in Todd Gitlin, *The Whole World is Watching* (Berkeley: University of California Press, 2003), p. 280.

39 Wright Mills, *The Power Elite*, p. 302.

40 Ibid., p. 303.

41 Ibid., p. 304.

42 Ibid.

43 Modern arguments against Mills' pessimism that turn on new technology do not convince, given the very small audiences that most individuals can reach, much less influence. Besides a public that does not meet face to face can only engage in a very thin form of communication.

5 Neoliberal Publics

1 Leonard Silk and David Vogel, *Ethics and Profits: The Crisis of Confidence in American Business* (New York: Simon and Schuster, 1976), p. 72.

2 Ibid., p. 130.

3 Sharon Beder, *Free Market Missionaries: The Corporate Manipulation of Community Values* (London: Earthscan, 2006), p. 33.

4   Reagan's Inaugural Address, 20 January 1981.

5   Silk and Vogel, *Ethics and Profits*, p. 77.

6   Ibid., p. 49.

7   Michel J. Crozier, Samuel P. Huntington, Joji Watanuki, *The Crisis of Democracy* (New York: New York University Press, 1975), p. 8.

8   Ibid., p. 61.

9   Ibid., p. 6.

10 Ibid., p. 8.

11 Students for a Democratic Society, *The Port Huron Statement* (New York: Students for a Democratic Society, 1964), pp. 7–8.

12 Ibid., p. 49.

13 James Kirkpatrick Davis, *Assault on the Left* (Westport: Praeger, 1997), pp. 8, 25. Any attempt to understand the history of the struggle to develop an independent left in the period after 1945 must take into account the active role of the UK and US states in encouraging activists down a series of blind alleys.

14 Philip Lesly, *The People Factor: Managing the Human Climate* (Homewood: Dow Jones-Irwin Inc, 1974), p. 261.

15 Howard Zinn, *A People's History of the United States* (New York: Harpercollins, 2001), p. 541.

16 Beder, *Free Market Missionaries*, p. 74.

17 Lesly, *The People Factor*, p. 6.

18 Crozier et al., *The Crisis of Democracy*, p. 113.

19 Quoted in M. N. S. Sellers, *American Republicanism* (New York: New York University Press, 1994), pp. 106–7.

20 Crozier et al., *The Crisis of Democracy*, pp. 113–14. Emphasis added.

21 See, for example, Anna Minton, *Ground Control: Fear and Happiness in the Twenty-First Century City* (London: Penguin, 2009). The author notes how non-market factors gradually vanished from definitions of the public interest in Britain from 1979 onwards.

22 Quoted in Simon Clarke, 'The Neoliberal Theory of Society', in Alfredo Saad-Filho and Deborah Johnston (eds.), *Neoliberalism: A Critical Reader* (London: Pluto, 2005), p. 51.

23 Ronald C. Moe, 'Governance Principles', in *Making Government Manageable* (Baltimore: Johns Hopkins Press, 2004), p. 30. The phrase is Dennis Mueller's.

24 Leys, *Market-Driven Politics*, p. 39.

25 Massimo Florio, *The Great Divestiture* (London: MIT Press, 2004), pp. 341–2.

26 Ibid., p. 352.

27 Kjell A. Eliassen and Nick Sitter, *Understanding Public Management* (London: Sage, 2008), p. 101.

28 The collapse of the public service ethos coincided with a disastrous decline in the quality of official prose. The mandarin style did not outlive the mandarin.

29 Will Hutton, *The State We're In* (London: Vintage, 1996), pp. 92–3.

30 Tony Blair, quoted in Leys, *Market-Driven Politics*, p. 39. Leys's work provides a valuable insight into the process by which public services have been re-imagined as commodities that can be delivered to customers by profit-seeking companies.

31 Quoted in Richard Cockett, *Thinking the Unthinkable* (London: Fontana, 1995), pp. 272–5.

32 In the event much of the windfall from North Sea oil was spent on welfare payments to those made unemployed in the early eighties.

33 Sure enough, growth in Britain was slower in the 1980s than in the 1970s.

34 Harold Myerson, 'Class Warrior', *Washington Post*, 9 June 2004.

35 See Thomas Frank, *The Wrecking Crew: The American Right and the Lust for Power* (London: Random House, 2008), for a dissection of the intelligence business after 2001.

36 David Osborne and Ted Gaebler, *Reinventing Government* (New York: Plume, 1993), p. 325. See also p. 43 for their endorsement of Harlan Cleveland's view that 'we would do well to glory in the blurring of the public and private and not keep trying to draw a disappearing line in the water'.

37 Ibid., front cover blurb.

38   Office of Domestic Policy, 'A Revolution in Government', 3 March 1993.

39   Eric Lichtbau, 'Minting Bank Lobbyists on Capitol Hill', *New York Times*, 13 April 2010.

40   Eliassen and Sitter, *Understanding Public Management*, p. 93.

41   Anthony Barnett, 'We Must be Freed for this Elective Dictatorship', *Financial Times*, 20 October 1998.

42   Tony Blair, 'Modernising Public Services', speech to the Charter Mark Awards, Central Hall, 26 January 1999; http://archive. cabinetoffice.gov.uk

43   Tony Wood, 'Good Riddance to New Labour', *New Left Review* 62, March–April, 2010, p. 15.

44   Colin Leys, *Total Politics: Market Politics, Market State* (Monmouth: Merlin Press, 2008), p. 100.

45   Wood, 'Good Riddance to New Labour', p. 16.

46   Florio, *The Great Divestiture*, p. 196.

47   Leys, *Total Politics*, p. 99.

48   J. A. Hobson, *The Psychology of Jingoism* (London: Grant Richards, 1901), p. 84.

49   Quoted in Conrad Lodziak, *Manipulating Needs: Capitalism and Culture* (London: Pluto, 1995), pp. 75–6.

50   BBC website, 'Clarke Criticised Over Classics', 31 January 2003; http://news.bbc.co.uk

51   Polly Curtis, 'Universities Overhaul Will Make Them More Inclusive, Says Mandelson', *Guardian*, 3 November 2009.

52   David Rothkopf, *Superclass: The Global Power Elite and the World They Are Making* (New York: Farrar, Straus and Giroux, 2008), p.121.

53   Bernard Porter, 'Other People's Mail', *London Review of Books*, 19 November 2009. A book that advocates employee-ownership and financial sector reform presumably qualifies as a subversive document.

54   Philip Bobbitt, *The Shield of Achilles* (London: Penguin, 2002), p. 912.

55   Ibid., p. 667.

56   Walter Wriston, *The Twilight of Sovereignty* (New York: Macmillan, 1992), p. 67.

57 David M. Jones, *The Politics of Money* (New York: Simon and Schuster, 1991), p. 52. Jones thought this 'market Darwinism' was a good thing, since it 'usually produced the brightest and best Fed Chairman'. It produced Alan Greenspan.

58 Thomas Friedman, *The Lexus and the Olive Tree* (London: Harpercollins, 2000), p. 478.

59 Martin Wolf, *Why Globalization Works* (London: Yale University Press, 2005), p. 298. Wolf has not, as far as I'm aware, repeated the point since 2007.

6 The Outlines of the Crisis

1   Curran and Seaton, *Power without Responsibility*, pp. 87–90.

2   President George Bush, Address to a Joint Session of Congress, 20 September 2001.

3   Richard Sennett, *The Fall of Public Man* (New York: Knopf, 1977), p. 25.

4   Ibid., pp. 281–2.

5   Quoted in Jacques Barzun, *The House of Intellect* (New York: Harper Torchbooks, 1959), p. 56.

6   'Transcript: Rick Davis on "Fox News Sunday"', 7 September 2008; http://www.foxnews.com

7   Amy Chozick, 'Desirée Rogers: Brand Obama', *Wall Street Journal*, 30 April 2009.

8   Mark Sweney, 'Barack Obama Campaign Claims Two Top Prizes at Cannes Lion Ad Awards', *Guardian*, 29 June 2009.

9   BBC News online, 'Full Text of Blair Memo', 17 July 2000; http://news.bbc.co.uk

10 Quoted in Berle and Means, *The Modern Corporation and Private Property*, p. 352.

11 Christopher Simpson, *National Security Directives of the Reagan and Bush Administrations* (Boulder: Westview, 1995), p. 304.

12 Quoted in Robin Ramsay, *The Rise of New Labour* (Harpenden: Pocket Essentials, 2002), p. 90.

13 Paul Dacre, 'Speech to the Society of Editors', 9 November 2008; www.pressgazette.co.uk

14 Wright Mills, *White Collar*, p. xvii.

7   Estranged From the World

1 'Richard Cheney: Saddam Hussein is a Danger to World Peace', *Independent*, 28 August 2002.

2 'How the Language Over Weapons of Mass Destruction Changed', *Telegraph*, 11 July 2003.

3 Craig Unger, 'The War They Wanted, The Lies They Needed', *Vanity Fair*, July 2006.

4 Charles Lewis and Mark Reading-Smith, 'The War Card', 23 January 2008; available at http://projects.publicintegrity.org

5 Friedrich Nietzsche, *Untimely Meditations* (Cambridge: Cambridge University Press, 1998), p. 190.

6 Quoted in Tariq Ali, *Rough Music* (London: Verso, 2005), pp. 90–1.

7 *USA Today*, 6 September 2003; Zogby International, 28 February 2006; http://zogby.com

8 'The Times and Iraq', *New York Times*, 26 May 2004.

9 Joan Didion, *Political Fictions* (New York: Knopf, 2001), p. 43.

10 Paul Krugman, 'Supply-Side Virus Strikes Again', *Slate*, 16 August 1996.

11 John Cassidy, 'Anatomy of a Meltdown', *New Yorker*, 1 December 2008.

12 The US magazine *Monthly Review* consistently flagged up the dangers of the neoliberal model. See John Bellamy Foster and Fred Magdoff, *The Great Financial Crisis: Causes and Consequences* (New York: Monthly Review Press, 2009).

13 Peter Warburton, *Debt and Delusion* (London: Penguin), 1999, p. 261.

14 Ann Pettifor, *The Coming First World Debt Crisis* (Houndsmill: Palgrave, 2006).

15 Julie Fishman-Lapin, 'Prophet of Doom?', *The Stamford-Nowalk Advocate*, 6 August 2006.

16 'Geithner Reassures Market Over Credit Risk', *Financial Times*, 12 May 2005.

17 'Bond Risk Falls After Bernanke Comments, Default Swaps Show', www.bloomberg.com, 28 February 2007.

18 'HSBC Warning', *Financial Times*, 8 February 2007.

19 Andrew Hill, 'Pym's Successor Must Change Gear at A&L', *Financial Times*, 21 February 2007.

20 Chris Brown-Humes, 'Speculative Mania Drives London Markets High', *Financial Times*, 11 May 2007.

21 Richard Lambert, speech at the Reform Media Group Dinner, 2 December 2008; www.cbi.org.uk

22 Dean Baker, 'Midsummer Meltdown', Center for Economic and Policy Research, August 2007; available at: http://www.cepr.net

23 Brian Stelter, 'A.P. Says It Wants to Know Everything About Britney Spears', *New York Times*, 14 January 2008.

24 Archive search on 25 November 2009; http://www.ap.org

25 Bertram Gross, *Friendly Fascism: The New Face of Power in America* (Montreal: Black Rose Books, 1985), p. 207.

26 Jeremy Warner, 'Oligarchs, Mandelson and Osborne', *Independent*, 22 October 2008.

27 Iain Watson, 'Corfu Questions Linger for Mandelson', BBC News online, 28 October 2008; http://news.bbc.co.uk

28 In competitive markets whatever is possible becomes necessary. Absent effective regulation and oversight enterprise tends to take on a criminal character. Michael Smith, 'Banks Financing Mexico Gangs Admitted in Wells Fargo Deal', 29 June 2010, Bloomsberg; bloomberg.com

29 By way of comparison, in the same period British newspapers mentioned the singer Dennis Lotis more than 20 times. LOTIS is part of International Financial Services, London, which used to be called British Invisibles.

30 'Lord Brittan Chairs LOTIS', *Financial Times*, 9 February 2001. It seems that Lord Brittan had taken up the post of chair of the 'High-Level LOTIS Group', an even more esoteric-sounding organization.

31 See the International Financial Services, London (IFSL) website: www.ifsl.org.uk

32 Liberalisation of Trade in Services (LOTIS) Committee, 'Minutes of Meeting Held on Thursday, 22 February 2001 at Lloyd's, One Lime Street, London EC3', available at www.corpwatch.org

33 Quoted by Greg Philo in 'Television, Politics, and the New Right', available at www.gla.ac.uk

34 Graham Paterson, 'Alan Greenspan Claims Iraq War was Really for Oil', *The Times*, 16 September 2007.

35 Robert Reich, 'Corporate Power in Overdrive', *New York Times*, 18 March 2001.

8   Estranged From Each Other

1   Benjamin I. Page with Marshall M. Bouton, *The Foreign Policy Disconnect: What Americans Want from Our Leaders but Don't Get* (Chicago: University of Chicago Press, 2006), p. 17.

2   Lawrence R. Jacobs and Benjamin I. Page, 'Who Influences U.S. Foreign Policy?', *American Political Science Review* 99, pp. 107–23, quoted in ibid., p. 222.

3   Gardiner Harris, 'In American Health Care, Drug Shortages are Chronic', *New York Times*, 31 October 2004.

4   The polling data come from Paul Street, 'Health Reform: Theirs and Ours', *ZNet*, 24 March 2010.

5   Justin Lewis, *Constructing Public Opinion: How Political Elites Do What They Like and Why We Seem to Go Along With It* (New York: Columbia University Press, 2001), p. 200.

6   John McGuire, 'Well, Come On Down!', *St Louis Post-Despatch*, 20 July 1997.

7   Newsquest search, 13 January 2009. See Amy Harmon, 'Flying Saucer Buffs to Market Half Century of Hazy History', *New York Times*, 14 June 1997.

8   'Help Wanted', *USA Today*, 14 March 1996, and Stephen H. Dunphy, 'The Newsletter', *Seattle Times*, 28 March 1996.

9   Richard Harwood, 'Making Sense of Campaigns', *Washington Post*, 24 August 1996.

10 Claudia H. Deutsch, 'New Surveys Show That Big Business Has a P.R. Problem', *New York Times*, 9 December 2005.

11 Page and Bouton, *The Foreign Policy Disconnect*, p. 309, n. 19.

12 Quoted in John Carey, *The Intellectual and the Masses* (London: Faber and Faber, 1992), p. 25.

13 David O. Sear and Carolyn L. Funk, 'Self-Interest in Americans' Political Opinions', in Jane J. Mansbridge (ed.), *Beyond Self-Interest* (Chicago: Chicago University Press, 1990), p. 170.

14 *Power to the People: An Independent Inquiry into Britain's Democracy* (York: The Power Inquiry), p. 167.

15 Ibid., Executive Summary, p. 6.

16 Steve Richards, 'She May Have Done Nothing Wrong, But Our Political Culture Will Destroy Tessa Jowell', *Independent*, 2 March 2006.

17 Onora O'Neill, *A Question of Trust* (Cambridge: Cambridge University Press, 2002), p. 13. O'Neill makes no distinction between civil servants, professionals and private employees in her discussion. The idea that a civil servant might be more reliable than a corporate employee in certain contexts doesn't appear to occur to her.

18 All quotes attributed to Mark Thompson are taken from his speech 'The Trouble with Trust: Building Confidence in Institutions', 15 January 2008; available at: www.bbc.co.uk/pressoffice

19 Thompson felt no need to offer data in support of this assertion.

20 Steven Cohen and William Eimicke, *The New Effective Public Manager* (San Francisco: Jossey-Bass, 1995), p. 316.

21 BBC News online, 'Blair on the Media', 12 June 2007; http://news.bbc.co.uk

22 '"Remember what happened the last time you shouted like that", I asked the spin doctor', Nick Robinson, *The Times*, 16 July 2004. See also the discussion of Nick Robinson's remarks on the Medialens website: www.medialens.org

23 Pierre Bourdieu, *Political Interventions* (London: Verso, 2008), p. 327.

9   Estranged From Ourselves

1 Quoted in Richard Layard, *Has Social Science a Clue?* (London: Centre for Economic Performance, 2003), p. 50.

2 Immanuel Kant, *Critique of Practical Reason*, trans. Thomas Kingsmill Abbott, (Mineola: Dover, 2004), p. 170.

3 Berle and Means, *The Modern Corporation and Private Property*, p. 349.

4 Quoted in Christopher Lasch, *The Revolt of the Elites and the Betrayal of Democracy* (New York: Norton, 1995), p. 78.

5 Quoted in Robin McKie, 'The Ant King's Last Mission', *Observer*, 1 October 2006.

6 Steven Pinker, 'This Much I Know', *Observer*, 22 June 2008.

7 Consider whether a seventeenth-century political philosopher transported to Montreal in the middle of the strike would have stolen a television set.

8 Richard Dawkins, *The Selfish Gene* (Oxford: Oxford University Press, 2006), p. 278.

9 Bruce E. Levine, *Surviving America's Depression Epidemic* (White River Junction: Chelsea Green Publishing, 2007), p. 172.

10 Alcohol Needs Assessment Research Project (ANARP): The 2004 national alcohol needs assessment for England, 1 November 2005; available at www.dh.gov.uk

11 'Statistics on Drug Misuse: England, 2009', The Health and Social Care Information Centre, 26 November 2009; available at www. ic.nhs.uk

12 Office for National Statistics, 'Mental Health: 1 in 6 Adults Have a Neurotic Disorder', 17 January 2006; available at www.statistics.gov.uk

13 Richard Wilkinson and Kate Pickett, *The Spirit Level:Why More Equal Societies Almost Always Do Better* (London: Allen Lane, 2009), p. 35.

14 Kwame McKenzie and Trudy Harpham (eds.), *Social Capital and Mental Health* (London: Jessica Kingsley Publishers, 2006), p. 8.

15 Minton, *Ground Control*, p. 177.

16 Robert Greene, *The 48 Laws of Power* (London: Profile, 2000).

17 Rhonda Byrne, *The Secret* (London: Simon and Schuster, 2006).

18 Quoted in William Leach, *Land of Desire: Merchants, Power and the Rise of a New American Culture* (New York: Vintage, 1994), p. 229.

19 Heath quoted in Jonathan Franzen, *How To Be Alone* (London: Harpercollins, 2002), pp. 81–2.

10 Public Commissioning

1 Lasch, *The Revolt of the Elites and the Betrayal of Democracy*, p. 12.

2 Niccolò Machiavelli, *The Prince* (London: Penguin, 1999), pp. 6, 99.

3 Michael Schudson, 'What Public Journalism Knows About Journalism But Doesn't Know About Public', in Theodore L. Glasser (ed.), *The Idea of Public Journalism* (New York: Guilford, 1999), p. 119. Schudson is summarizing Jay Rosen.

4 J. A. Hobson, *The Psychology of Jingoism* (London: Grant Richards, 1901), p. 115.

5 Harrington, *The Commonwealth of Oceana*, p. 18.

6 Robert McChesney and John Nichols, *The Death and Life of American Journalism: The Media Revolution That Will Begin the World Again* (Philadelphia: Nation Books, 2010), pp. 201–6.

7 I worry that by directing subsidy to existing institutions the voucher scheme will give an unjustifiable advantage to those who already have a brand or to those who are able to build one through foundation support. Given the role of foundations in neutering social science they can hardly be trusted to sponsor a genuinely effective free press. Nevertheless, the key point remains: we agree on the pressing need for direct citizen participation in the distribution of funds to the media.

8   See the discussion in Chapter 7 above.

9   BBC, 'Full Financial and Governance Statements, 2008/09', p. 25; available at http://downloads.bbc.co.uk

10   'Digital Britain', June 2009, p. 143 and passim; available at www.culture.gov.uk

11   Speech by Ed Richards, 28 April 2009; available at www.ofcom.org.uk

12   I am indebted to Paul Lashmar for this estimate.

13   That said, the system I propose would lead to rapid change to the libel laws in the UK, once the population as a whole grasp the extent to which they hamper publication of the information required for self-government.

14   See Jonathan Githens-Mazer and Robert Lambert, 'Islamophobia and Anti-Muslim Hate Crime: a London Case Study', 28 January 2010; available at http://centres.exeter.ac.uk

15   'Communications Act of 1934', SEC 303 [47 U.S.C. 303]; available at http://www.fcc.gov

16   'Text of President Clinton's 1998 State of the Union Address', 27 January 1998, Congressional Record; available at www.washingtonpost.com

17   See Charles Lewis, 'Commentary: Profiteering from Democracy', 30 August 2000, Center for Public Integrity; available at www.publicintegrity.org

18   Michael Schudson and Leonard Downie, 'The Reconstruction of American Journalism', *Columbia Journalism Review*, 10 October 2009, p. 72.

19   Associated Press, 'Pentagon Sets its Sights on Public Opinion', 5 February 2009; available at www.msnbc.msn.com

20   See Thomas Ferguson, *Golden Rule: The Investment Theory of Party Competition and the Logic of Money-Driven Political Systems* (Chicago: University of Chicago Press, 1995), for an account of the ways in which major investors can screen out policies that they dislike, even when they are favoured by large majorities.

21   This reached a kind of perfection in 2004 when President Bush won a second term by 'defending marriage' and then tried to privatize social security.

11 A Public System of Knowledge

1 Joseph Stiglitz's comments are taken from the website of the Institute for New Economic Thinking: www.ineteconomics.org

2 Philip Augar, 'It is Time to Put Finance in its Box', *Financial Times*, 14 April 2009.

3 Donald Fisher, *Fundamental Development of the Social Sciences: Rockefeller Philanthropy and the United States Social Science Research Council* (Ann Arbor: University of Michigan Press, 1993), p. 238.

4 Quoted in ibid., p. 71.

5 Christopher Simpson, *The Science of Coercion* (New York: Oxford University Press, 1994).

6 See Herbert Schiller, *Culture, Inc.: The Corporate Takeover of Public Expression* (New York: Oxford University Press, 1989).

7 Henry Kissinger, *American Foreign Policy: Three Essays* (London: Weidenfeld and Nicolson, 1969), p. 28. See also Dean Baker, 'Midsummer Meltdown', August 2007, Center for Economic and Policy Research, available at www.cepr.net.

8 Thomas MacGarity and Wendy Wagner, *Bending Science* (Cambridge: Harvard University Press, 2008), pp. 156–64. The book provides a valuable summary of the various ways in which interested parties interfere in the conduct and reception of scientific research.

9 Harvey Brooks, *The Government of Science* (Cambridge, MA: MIT Press, 1968), p. 23.

10 Ibid., p. 23. Though Brooks doesn't say so, the Americans also benefited greatly from the talents of mostly Jewish Europeans fleeing fascism. After the war they also took steps to benefit from the talents of fascists fleeing from Europe.

11 Jeff Schmidt, *Disciplined Minds: A Critical Look at Salaried Professionals and the Soul-battering System That Shapes Their Identities* (New York: Rowman and Littlefield, 2000), p. 59.

12 Intersociety Working Group, 'Report XXVIII: Research and

Development FY 2004', American Association for the Advancement of Science, 2003; available at http://www.aaas.org

13 'Joint Vision 2020: America's Vision – Preparing for Tomorrow', June 2000; available at www.dtic.mil. Imperialism and capitalism have distinct, though complementary, conceptions of the sublime. The one is captivated by the dream of perfect domination; the other by the prospect of pure profit.

14 'Remarks as Delivered by Secretary of State Donald H. Rumsfeld', 10 September 2001; available at www.defense.gov

15 See, for example, Thomas Frank, *The Wrecking Crew* (London: Random House, 2008), for an eye-watering account of the way that tax dollars become income for private contractors.

16 Space Command's 'Vision for 2020' can be accessed online at www.fas.org. As far as I can tell it is an official document, though it appears to have been designed by a lunatic. It is also undated.

17 See Nick Turse, *The Complex: How the Military Invades Everyday Lives* (London: Faber and Faber, 2008), and Doug Rushkoff, *Coercion: The Professional Persuaders and Why We Listen* (London: Little, Brown, 1998).

18 See Schmidt, *Disciplined Minds*, especially pp. 59–64.

19 See Susan Mayor, 'NHS agrees to price reduction for prescription drugs for next five years', 13 November 2004, available at www.bmj.com.

20 Gillian Merron's answer to a question from Hugh Bailey, 'how much Government funding has been allocated to medical research in each year since 1996–97'. Merron replied that 'government funding for medical research is provided principally through the Department's national health service research and development budget and the Medical Research Council'. The £1.6 billion figure comes from the combined total for these principal sources of funds. See www.parliament.the-stationery-office.co.uk

21 See Irving Kirsch, *The Emperor's New Drugs* (London: The Bodley Head, 2009).

22 Walter Lippmann, *Public Opinion*, p. 251.

23 'Benefits cheat who claimed she could not work is caught out . . . after winning darts tournament', *Daily Mail*, 25 July 2009.

24 I suggest that the £2.3 billion that drug companies currently take from NHS payments for branded drugs and direct towards internal research and development should be used as the basis for public commissioning of scientific research.

25 See Dean Baker, 'The Myth of Market Fundamentalism', *Counterpunch*, 7 April 2010.

26 Richard Layard, 'Happiness: Has Social Science a Clue?', text of the Lionel Robbins Memorial Lectures, 25 February 2003, Lecture 3, p. 9; available at http://cep.lse.ac.uk

12 Reforming the Private Sector

1 Lasch, *The Revolt of the Elites and the Betrayal of Democracy*, p. 163.

2 Henry Augustine Washington (ed.), *The Writings of Thomas Jefferson*, Vol. VII (Washington: Taylor and Maury, 1854), p. 448.

3 Quoted in Naomi Klein, *The Shock Doctrine* (London: Penguin, 2008), p. 299. Klein notes that 'in 2003, the Bush administration spent $327 billion on contracts to private companies – nearly 40 cents of every discretionary dollar' (p. 301).

4 See Barbara Ehrenreich, *Smile or Die: How Positive Thinking Fooled America and the World* (London: Granta, 2009), for an account of the connection between self-absorption and corporate culture. See also Wright Mills, *White Collar*; Christopher Lasch, *The Culture of Narcissism: American Life in an Age of Diminishing Expectations* (New York: Norton, 1991); and Richard Sennett, *The Culture of the New Capitalism* (New Haven: Yale University Press, 2006).

5 Berle and Means, *The Modern Corporation and Private Property*, p. 352.

6 'The Banking Revolution', *The Economist*, 18 September 1971, quoted in Robin Ramsay, *The Rise of New Labour* (Harpenden: Pocket Essentials, 2002), p. 14.

7   Quoted in Jonathon Porritt, *Capitalism as if the World Matters* (London: Earthscan, 2007), p. 191. David Harvey has recently pointed out that it is at the point of contact between central banks and the large financial institutions that the distinction between state and economic power blurs – it marks the permanent blurring of the public and the private. See 'The Enigma of Capital', 26 April 2010; www.lse.ac.uk

Conclusion

1   There is another story to be told about how the classical idea of the public was first used to undermine feudalism in the interests of absolutism, but this falls outside the scope of an account that is unashamedly both partial and partial.

2   By 'economy of knowledge' I mean roughly who knows and who doesn't know what, how much it costs the first group to know, and how much it costs to deprive the second group of that knowledge.

3   Hobson, *The Psychology of Jingoism*, p. 138.

4   Nick Davies, *Flat Earth News: An Award-Winning Reporter Exposes Falsehood, Distortion and Propaganda in the Global Media* (London: Random House, 2008); McChesney and Nichols, *The Death and Life of American Journalism*.

5   See, especially, Sennett, *The Fall of Public Man*, pp. 337–40.

6   As government becomes ever more attentive to the demands of established power its language becomes ever more hyperbolic; see for example Al Gore's 'revolution in government' in 1993 and Nick Clegg's recent claim that the UK coalition government's constitutional proposals amount to the 'biggest shakeup of our democracy since 1832'.

7   See Don Slater, 'Public Private', in Chris Jenks (ed.), *Core Sociological Distinctions* (London: Sage, 1998), p. 148.

8   Bourdieu, *Political Interventions*, p. 338.

9   McChesney and Nichols, *The Death and Life of American Journalism*, p. 74.

Index

181–2; neoliberal restructuring 83–5; New Labour 88–91; opium trade 49; pharmaceutical industry 182–3; political culture 17–30, 37–47; political economy review 127–8; political imagination 6; the political nation 31–5; political participation 32, 35; populism 128; post-war boom 53; post-war settlement 98; privatization 84; public commissioning proposals 164–5; republicanism 18–30, 35, 201; restoration of the monarchy 31; rise of the public servant 48–58; ruling elite 32–4; Second World War 142–3; settlement of North America 43, 59; substance abuse 141; the Treasury 99; Tudor 18; TV license fee 164–5; unemployment 85; universal male suffrage 52; Victorian 49–51
Great Divestiture, The (Florio) 84
Great Society, the 62, 68–9, 99
Great Stink of 1858, the 50
Greece, classical 15
Greenspan, Alan 2, 92, 111, 118–9
Gross, Bertram 114

Habermas, Jürgen 5, 36–9
Harling, Philip 48
Harrington, James 18–9, 19, 22, 23, 25, 30, 60, 162
Harwood, Richard 125–6
health services 88, 89
Heath, Shirley Brice 147–8
Hobbes, Thomas 18, 24–6, 28, 139
Hobson, J. A. 160–1, 203
Homer, Sidney 34
Hood, Stuart 55
Hoskyns, John 85
Hubbard, Al 111–2
human nature 7–8, 47, 98; competitive individualism 138–44; and inequality 142–4; public choice theory 83
human relationships, impersonal 62, 68–9
Hume, David 31–2, 40–2, 44, 172

Huntington, Samuel 79–80, 81–2, 83
Hutton, Will 85

illiberal actions 27–8
impartiality 55–6
imperialism 43
independence, material 29–30
India 59–60
individual distinction 70
individuals: enlightened 44–7; lack of knowledge of other 135; solitary 145–9
industrialization 50, 62, 69, 71
inequality 29, 142–4, 146, 164, 206
information. *See also* knowledge: access 155; production of 9–10; reform 157–8; reliable 157
injustice 174
institutions, participatory 46–7, 206
intellectual autonomy 41–2
interest groups 71–4, 75
International Monetary Fund 112
international trade 197
intimate life, media invasion of 104–6, 113–4, 202–3
investigative researchers, public commissioning 165–6
Iraq, invasion of 6–7, 107–10, 118–9, 120
It's a Wonderful Life (film) 70
ITV 164

Jaggers, Neil 117
James II, King 33
Jefferson, Thomas 60
Johnson, Lyndon Baines 116
Johnson, Samuel 42
Jones, David M. 92
Joseph Rowntree Charitable Trust 127–8
Joseph Rowntree Reform Trust 127–8
journalism: accountability 160–3; citizen 157–8, 162, 173; collapse in standards 110–1; deskilled 204; failures in reporting 107; invasion of intimate life 104–6; public 38–9, 158, 160–2;

..
Index

Paulson, Hank 3
Paulson, John 112
pension funds 198
Pentagon, the 169, 179–80, 184
personality, commodification of 106
Pettifor, Ann 112
Phantom Public, The (Lippmann) 65
pharmaceutical industry 182–3, 186–7
physical science 177–9
Pickett, Kate 142
Pinker, Steven 139
Platonism 53, 60
pluralism 71–4, 74–5, 77, 119; cultural 90
policy formation, Lippmann's critique
    63–4
policy objectives 66
political activism 79–81
political economy 40–2
political identity 4, 17
political participation 32, 35, 146, 158–9
political process, media scrutiny 132
politicians: expenses scandal 132,
    157; and financial magnates 115–6;
    marketing of personalities 99–100,
    101–3, 172; media hostility 131–2; and
    organized crime 116
popular culture 134
popular preferences, and policy 123–7
popular representation, undermined 99
popular sovereignty, Lippmann's critique
    62–6
populism 126–7, 128
Port Huron Statement, The (Students for a
    Democratic Society) 80–1
Porter, Bernard 47, 91
positive liberty 26–8
positive thinking 145–8
power: centre of 71; collective 19, 206;
    coordinating 73; corporate 193–4;
    illegitimate 23; limits 28; military 4;
    private 16–7, 20–1; relationships of
    197, 208; right to 41; shared 21; and
    the state 24–6
PR Reporter 81
prejudice 127, 192

Prince, The (Machiavelli) 156
private actors 47
private enterprise 78–9
private finance initiatives 88–9
private foundations 176–7
private institutions 155–6, 173
private life, right to 203
private sector reforms 191–200;
    employee ownership 196–7; financial
    sector 197–9; limited liability 194–6
private world 4, 5; relation to public
    40–2, 50–2, 207
privatization 84
property 28, 34, 41, 43, 50, 78
pseudo-environment, the 63
psychological Darwinism 139–44
psychological warfare 104, 170
psychology 67
public, the: classical 15–30; definition
    4–6, 34–5, 43–4; distinction from
    the mass 75–6; role 39–40; traditions
    201–2
public actors 47
public appointments 48
public choice theory 83
Public Citizen reports 87
public commissioning 9–12, 153–74,
    191–2, 205–9; in America 168–70;
    benefits 158–9, 173–4, 188–9;
    Citizenship News Voucher scheme
    162–3; civic engagement 172;
    comparison with public journalism
    160–2; description 158; distribution
    of results 160; and the electoral
    process 170; equality 167; funding
    159–60, 164–7, 169–70, 173,
    187–8, 189; investigative researchers
    165–6; journalism 158, 166–7, 208;
    knowledge 191, 207–8; resource
    allocation 159–60; science 185–90;
    social science 187–8; vulnerability 167
public conscience, the 51
public diplomacy 104, 170
public good, the 8, 44, 52
public health 50, 189

243